TALLEY & SON

TALLEY & SON

A Play in Two Acts

LANFORD WILSON

A MERMAID DRAMABOOK

Hill and Wang   *New York*
A division of Farrar, Straus and Giroux

For Bruce McCarty

An earlier draft of *Talley & Son* (then called *A Tale Told*) was first produced by Circle Repertory Company, in New York City, during their 1980/81 season.

The cast:

VIOLA PLATT /	Nancy Kilmer
OLIVE /	Patricia Wettig
NETTA /	Helen Stenborg
LOTTIE /	Elizabeth Sturges
ELDON /	Michael Higgins
BUDDY /	Timothy Shelton
EMMET YOUNG /	Lindsey Ginter
HARLEY CAMPBELL /	Jimmie Ray Weeks
MR. TALLEY /	Fritz Weaver
AVALAINE PLATT /	Laura Hughes
TIMMY /	David Ferry
SALLY /	Trish Hawkins

Directed by Marshall W. Mason
Production Stage Manager: Fred Reinglas

Talley & Son was first produced by Circle Repertory Company, in Saratoga Springs, New York, at the Little Theater, Saratoga Performing Arts Center, July 8, 1985. The play opened in New York City at Circle Repertory Company's theater on November 22, 1985.

The cast:

VIOLA PLATT /	Lisa Emery
OLIVE /	Laura Hughes
NETTA /	Helen Stenborg
LOTTIE /	Joyce Reehling Christopher
ELDON /	Farley Granger
BUDDY /	Lindsey Richardson
EMMET YOUNG /	Steve Decker
HARLEY CAMPBELL /	Richard Backus
MR. TALLEY /	Edward Seamon
AVALAINE PLATT /	Julie Bargeron
TIMMY /	Robert MacNaughton
SALLY /	Trish Hawkins

Directed by Marshall W. Mason
Production Stage Manager: Jody Boese
Sets: John Lee Beatty
Costumes: Laura Crow
Lighting: Dennis Parichy
Sound: Chuck London Media/Stewart Werner

"Thou has set our iniquities before thee, our secret sins in the light of Thy countenance. For all our days are passed away in Thy wrath; we spend our years as a tale that is told."

Psalms 90

TALLEY & SON

THE TALLEYS

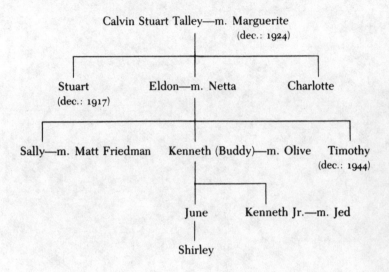

Calvin Stuart Talley—m. Marguerite
(dec.: 1924)

Stuart   Eldon—m. Netta   Charlotte
(dec.: 1917)

Sally—m. Matt Friedman   Kenneth (Buddy)—m. Olive   Timothy
(dec.: 1944)

June   Kenneth Jr.—m. Jed

Shirley

TIME

Independence Day, 1944

PLACE

The front parlor of the Talley Place; a farm near
Lebanon, Missouri

CHARACTERS

CALVIN STUART TALLEY, eighty.

LOTTIE TALLEY, his daughter, forty-five.

ELDON TALLEY, Talley's son, fifty-two.

NETTA TALLEY, Eldon's wife, the same age.

KENNETH (BUDDY) TALLEY, Eldon's son, twenty-nine. In the uniform of an Army Staff Sergeant.

OLIVE TALLEY, Buddy's wife, twenty-eight.

TIMMY TALLEY, Eldon's son, twenty. In Marine fatigues.

SALLY TALLEY, Eldon's daughter, thirty-one.

EMMET YOUNG, a handyman.

VIOLA PLATT, the washerwoman, thirty-five but looking older.

AVALAINE PLATT, her daughter, seventeen, looking older.

HARLEY CAMPBELL, Eldon's business partner, thirty-one.

ACT I

The formal parlor of the Talley place, a large and elegant farmhouse constructed in 1860, just outside Lebanon, Missouri.

On the upstage wall is a fireplace flanked by double sliding doors that open to a wide, imposing hallway, showing on one side the front door and at the other the entrance to the kitchen and dining room.

At stage left, large double doors open to a porch that surrounds the house; at stage right, matching doors of solid mahogany open to the office.

In one of the windows is a two-star flag indicating that the family has two sons in the war.

The room has been furnished luxuriously at (perhaps) the turn of the century. It is comfortable, if a little stiff, but verging on threadbare. The floor shines, the room is spotlessly clean.

The time is sunset, July 4, 1944.
TIMMY TALLEY *stands near the fireplace. He speaks to the* *audience.*

TIMMY: America won the Second World War today. It'll be August next year before anybody knows it, but we took Saipan, and from Saipan we'll take its little cousin island, Tinian, and from Tinian a B-29 can finally take off for Japan and get back again, and then the war's over. I'm a little early here. This is the Fourth of July; I'm due here on the sixth, for Granddad's funeral. I got my pass in my pocket. And while I'm here we're gonna have this big powwow about the family business. See, Harley Campbell and Dad own this garment factory, Talley and Son. Now some big company's wantin' to buy us out. Dad wrote me I'd better get my butt back here quick before Harley sold off everything but my stamp collection. (ELDON *comes in*) Hey, Dad, that was one hell of a fire-and-brimstone letter. Hey, could you look at me for a change? What you don't know—I got a letter from you and one from Harley and one from Mom. Dad? (ELDON *goes into the office.* TIMMY *looks back to the audience*) Last thing I knew I was bumping along on a stretcher, some guy's hand over my eyes. I was yelling, "I gotta see Dad, man, get me up. Everything going all right, I'm home for the sixth." I think everything didn't go all right.

(SALLY *runs down the stairs*)

LOTTIE: Sally. Sally. I thought you locked yourself in your room.

SALLY: Oh, I am so mad, I really am.

TIMMY: That's my sister.

LOTTIE: Sally, Buddy and Olive don't have the sense . . .

SALLY: Oh, I am very angry with both of them, and Mother, too.

LOTTIE: Mr. Friedman was as polite and gentlemanly as anyone could ask.

SALLY: Most of all I am angry with Matt Friedman.

LOTTIE: It wasn't Matt—

SALLY: How dare he get himself into a fight with my brother.

LOTTIE: Matt wasn't fighting; he was going to sit on the porch and wait for you. Buddy chased him off with a shotgun.

SALLY: Oh, Lord.

LOTTIE: I hit Buddy with a broom, and I'm glad.

SALLY: Why did Matt come down here in the first place? He knows how we feel about him. Oh!

LOTTIE: He said he wanted to talk to your father.

SALLY: Aunt Lottie, I wish you would get all that romantic twaddle out of your mind.

LOTTIE: Well–

SALLY: If there was a place to move to, I'd move there tonight.

LOTTIE: I know, darling.

OLIVE: (*Coming down the stairs*): Sally, I just got June to sleep. You're going to wake her right up.

SALLY: Well, I wouldn't want to do that.

LOTTIE: Where are you going, Sally?

SALLY: Out. Out. I'm going out.

LOTTIE: Sally, stay here and talk to me.

SALLY: I am very angry with this entire household. (*She slams out the door*)

LOTTIE (*At the door*): Sally!

TIMMY (*To audience*): I think my sister's very angry with this entire household.

LOTTIE (*Calling*): Sally, come back up here.

OLIVE: Aunt Lottie, you might have some consideration. You're going to wake June right up.

LOTTIE: I'm not speaking to you, Olive. (*She storms off outside, leaving* TIMMY *alone in the parlor*)

TIMMY: Boy, this family. This house. This room. This is where we always liked to come and play 'cause we weren't allowed to. We'd lay around on the rug playing Monopoly, but Sally'd always lose interest and I'd just lose—Buddy'd beat up on Sally and Sally's old boyfriend Harley'd beat up on Buddy and all three of them would beat up on me 'cause I was the youngest. About the only thing we did together was save up our dimes and sneak off down to the Lyric Theater to see a picture show, 'cause we weren't allowed to do that either. If the family ever went to the movies, they could watch us win the war next week on the Movietone Newsreel. They could see me die.

VIOLA (*Off, calling loudly*): Mr. Eldon? Anybody at home? Mrs. Talley?

OLIVE (*Upstairs, whispering; overlapping*): Viola, hush up. Oh, my goodness.

VIOLA (*Continuing*): Mr. Eldon?

TIMMY: Is anybody going to get the door?

VIOLA: Anybody to home here? Miss Charlotte?

OLIVE (*Continuing*): Oh, good Lord, would somebody shut that woman up. (NETTA *appears from the back hall*) Mother, I just got June to sleep. She's gonna wake her right up.

TIMMY: That's Mom.

NETTA: Why didn't you come around to the back, Viola?

VIOLA: I thought you'd all gone off to the celebration; I couldn't raise nobody.

OLIVE: Oh, good Lord, Viola, shush. I swear, yelling through the house to wake the dead.

NETTA: Olive's just trying to get the girl to sleep, Viola.

VIOLA: I was wondering if your husband was at home, Mrs. Talley.

NETTA: I don't know if Eldon's here or not. What is it? I'll tell him.

VIOLA: No, no, don't bother, ain't important.

LOTTIE (*Coming in from outside*): Damn her hide.

NETTA (*To* LOTTIE): I hope you are thoroughly ashamed of yourself after the spectacle you made here this afternoon.

LOTTIE: I'm not talking to you, Netta. (*She settles at a table where she will work crossword puzzles and play solitaire*)

NETTA: Lottie, now that we got rid of that Jew, I'd like Buddy to have one nice evening with the family. Nora and I are trying to cook supper for ten people, with Olive running in and out, in and out, in and out, in and out, and that's enough for me to put up with, thank you. Viola, I'll get the laundry; I've not even got it sorted yet.

VIOLA: I can do that.

NETTA: No, we don't want any more people parading through the house. It's all upside down. (*She exits*)

TIMMY: Mom's having a hard time out there. My big brother, Buddy, is home, too. He's on special leave, and Mom and the cook, Nora, are making him a welcome-home-soldier supper. The kitchen looks like a cyclone went through it.

VIOLA: Miss Talley, I got to talk to your brother, it's kinda important.

LOTTIE: I can't tell you where he is.

VIOLA: Well, I'll come back after I get the laundry to soak, 'cause I better talk to him.

LOTTIE: Can't it wait till tomorrow? You look done in.

VIOLA: No, no, it better not wait.

OLIVE (*Entering*): Well, I thought you'd slipped a cog and was talking to yourself. It's a miracle June went back to sleep with all that commotion. Does this room smell? I've had the windows opened all day; I think it still smells. I guess you heard my Buddy came home on leave last night—

VIOLA: I saw him, yes.

OLIVE: And Timmy gets home from the Pacific day after to-morrow, so we're all together for one day at least.

TIMMY: I guess I'm gonna miss the party.

OLIVE: We're all trying to have everything so perfect. I can't quit thinking they're sending Buddy right back to Italy Thursday morning. I swear my prayer is that the war ends this night and he doesn't have to go back at all.

VIOLA: He's been over to Italy?

OLIVE: You knew that. He was at the wheel of General Mark Clark's car last month when they drove the Krauts out of Rome. We wired him how his granddad was failing; General Clark wrote an order for Buddy to come home, right on the spot. Then, too, he'd got his arm hurt awful bad—(LOTTIE *snorts*)— so he couldn't drive. Lottie, he doesn't let on, but I can tell he's in terrible pain.

LOTTIE: He's General Clark's driver and he gets himself wounded during a victory celebration, falling down the Spanish steps.

OLIVE: They were under fire all winter, thank you. They sustained terrible casualties, Lottie. They only liberated Rome.

NETTA (*Entering with laundry*): Viola, come around to the back next time.

OLIVE: Mother, you ought to let me carry that.

NETTA: I'm sorry, Olive, don't call me Mother. It just makes me jump.

OLIVE: I'm sorry. I know.

NETTA: I can't visit—Nora and I are turning the goose. (*Exits to kitchen*)

OLIVE: I'm sorry. Did your folks put up any of that blackberry jam this year? That's the first thing Buddy asked for.

VIOLA: That's all gone.

OLIVE: Blackberry season's hardly over. I don't imagine you've had—

VIOLA: We sold all that.

OLIVE: Don't step there, honey, with those rubber soles. I'll be down on my hands and knees again all night.

VIOLA: You tell Mr. Eldon it's important that I talk to him.
OLIVE (*Overlapping some as* VIOLA *exits*): Don't yell in the hall; you'll wake— Don't go out that front door—you'll—(*Door slams*) I have never seen such a lack of the most basic social graces in my life. These cushions need recovering, don't they?

LOTTIE: Not tonight.

OLIVE: Aunt Lottie, there is no call for you to be catty.

LOTTIE: While you're bragging about Buddy and Timmy getting special leave, Mrs. Platt's brother Vaughan was killed in Cherbourg last week.

TIMMY: Vaughan was?

OLIVE: I don't think I know him.

TIMMY: Worked at the garage.

LOTTIE: He was that good-looking guy who used to pump gas for you.

OLIVE: Oh . . . Well, I'm sorry to hear that, but Viola Platt should be able to rejoice in another's fortune even in the midst of her own sorrow. I know the whole family is ignorant and distrustful, but I will not believe they're unfeeling. (*Sotto voce*) And her daughter, Avalaine Platt, has been seen with these eyes out with our handyman, Emmet Young, and I would not repeat the condition they were in. (*The office door opens,* ELDON *enters*) Oh, good Lord. I thought I'd seen a ghost.

ELDON: Hold on, there. My boy'd never forgive me if I gave his wife a heart attack.

OLIVE: I didn't even know we had a key to that office.

ELDON: We?

OLIVE: Well . . . anybody but Granddad.

ELDON: Thought it was about time we found out what Dad's been counting up in there all these years. Turns out we're a lot more comfortable than we thought we were, Sis. You ought to go out and buy a hat.

LOTTIE: No, it wouldn't set right on me, brother dear—you can buy the hat.

ELDON: I just might.

LOTTIE: Get a new pair of britches, too. You're getting too big for those.

OLIVE: I'm not saying I couldn't use a few new things.

ELDON: Would you look how radiant she is. One night with Buddy home and I never saw anyone looking . . . so well rested.

OLIVE: Dad!

ELDON: She's put on a frock, maybe even a brush of makeup?

OLIVE: No, I— Well, if I *had*, I guess I have good reason.

ELDON: You've got the parlor shining, too.

OLIVE: Mother and I thought we'd air it out. But it does seem so callous.

LOTTIE: Olive's getting the parlor ready for Papa's funeral— that ought to be quite a celebration.

OLIVE: Lottie, it's not like that at all.

ELDON: No, we just count our blessings and go on with what has to be done.

OLIVE (*At office door*): What's Mr. Talley been hiding in here?

ELDON: Hey!

OLIVE: Well, it's no business of mine. Dad, I'm fixing you and Buddy a little surprise for supper, so I'd better get crackin'. (*Exits*)

ELDON: I wish Olive wouldn't call me Dad.

LOTTIE: Did you see Sally on the road?

ELDON: Sally was the last thing I was looking for.

LOTTIE: The Talleys are up to their usual standard of hospitality this afternoon.

ELDON: How's that?

BUDDY (*Coming down from upstairs*): Olive, where did you say you put my house shoes?

OLIVE (*Off*): What, what?

NETTA (*Off*): What, what?

ELDON: Well, there's another country heard from.

TIMMY: Hey, Buddy.

BUDDY (*Looking into the room*): Hey, Dad, where you been? We had our fireworks early this Fourth.

NETTA (*Entering*): Eldon Talley, you have an absolute talent for leaving the house if you're going to be needed.

ELDON: What did I do this time?

BUDDY: He missed the fun, didn't he, Mom?

NETTA: I'll fun you.

BUDDY: You know that Jew you said Sally dragged home to supper last year? He came down from St. Louis for a visit.

ELDON: The hell you say.

NETTA: If he'd stayed ten minutes more, Sally would have driven up with him standing right there on the porch.

BUDDY: I took out that old shotgun; he started shaking like a hound shittin' razor blades.

NETTA (*Loving it*): I won't have that army-barracks talk in here.

BUDDY: You oughta seen him hightail it—

NETTA: Your sister was a lot of help, too.

BUDDY: Aunt Lottie, you still ticked at me?

LOTTIE: You want to talk to me, Buddy, you talk about something else.

BUDDY: I think Aunt Lottie's kinda sweet on him.

NETTA: Yelling Sally wanted to see him. That's just Sally being willful. She doesn't want to see that man.

LOTTIE: She came home from work at the hospital and everybody lit in on her like she—

NETTA: I am still her mother, I hope. And I know as well as I'm standing here that she brought that—man home last year just out of spite. I can't understand a word he says; I swear I think he's a Communist.

ELDON: Well, he's something.

NETTA: He *is*, he's a lunatic. I told Olive to call the sheriff, nobody could find you.

ELDON: I told you I was in town. Took advantage of the holiday to see what's going on down at Dad's bank.

BUDDY: That's all right, me and Harley gave him a fine reception.

ELDON: Yeah? And how come Harley to be here? Soon as I'm not?

BUDDY: How's that?

ELDON: I'll bet Harley didn't happen to mention how great it is that Delaware Industries wants to buy the factory either.

TIMMY: Delaware Industries! That's the company I was telling you about.

BUDDY: No, he said we ought to talk. Sounds interesting.

ELDON: Anyone'd think so to hear Harley tell it.

BUDDY: Interesting, interesting, that's all I said.

ELDON: Well, you and Harley can be interested all to hell and back, some people in the family aren't going to be that all-fired excited about selling out.

BUDDY: What's that supposed to mean?

NETTA: No business talk, now. You know how you two are.

ELDON: Your Harley's having pipe dreams about being on the board of some big corporation, sitting on his can smoking a cigar.

BUDDY: Heck, it's pretty hard to argue with getting paid for doing nothing.

ELDON: Oh, we'd get paid. The devil spends half his day just sitting down writing out checks.

BUDDY: You're so proud of Talley and Son—

ELDON: Damn right I am.

BUDDY: Well, you ought to be happy somebody's noticing it.

NETTA: Eldon, don't talk now—

OLIVE (*Entering*): Well, good morning sunshine in the middle of the afternoon. Did Viola wake you up, yelling for Dad?

BUDDY: I woke up because I was smelling Nora's Christmas goose. I could almost see the snowflakes flying.

OLIVE: You said you wanted to have Christmas on the Fourth of July. Did you have a good nap?

BUDDY: I slept like the dead once I finally got the chance.

OLIVE (*Thrilled*): Oh, don't say that! Oh! You! Oh! (*Playful to instantly serious*) Mother, do you think Granddaddy is strong enough to come to supper tonight?

LOTTIE: He'll be right at the head of the table.

ELDON: He was up this morning. Even managed to dress himself.

NETTA: We haven't seen him that strong in over a year.

BUDDY: Did you find those house shoes?

NETTA: I looked, Buddy, I think they might be gone.

BUDDY: They can't be gone, I've been dreaming about those shoes all through Italy.

OLIVE: Well, if we can't find them, we can surely buy you a new pair.

BUDDY: I don't want a new pair. I want my damn house shoes.

OLIVE: Well, they've taught you a few new words.

BUDDY: I told you to send them to Rome.

NETTA: We haven't got any of your mail from Rome yet.

OLIVE: I'm going to write to your company commander about all that censoring, too. They hardly touch Timmy's letters, they cut yours all to pieces.

BUDDY: Whata you hear from the fair-haired kid?

ELDON: Oh, we hit the jackpot yesterday.

NETTA: I got fifteen, Eldon got ten.

LOTTIE: I even got one.

NETTA: Lottie even got one.

ELDON: We really hit the jackpot.

BUDDY: I can't wait to see him, tell him to send his sister-in-law a grass skirt.

OLIVE: A sarong.

ELDON: I'll tell you. The Pacific sounds real disappointing in that department.

TIMMY: I didn't see one native female under sixty-five.

BUDDY: We don't always tell it all.

OLIVE: I didn't hear that.

BUDDY: Classified information.

OLIVE: Are you going to put on your shoes or are you going barefoot?

BUDDY: I was hoping to be able to put on my damn house shoes.

NETTA: Just don't be getting so free with that talk.

LOTTIE: Oh, shit

NETTA: Lottie, really!

LOTTIE: Everybody knows Olive burned those shoes last April.

OLIVE: Lottie Talley, when I do—I could even say, more than my share—I can't remember during spring cleaning if I might have accidentally thrown out—

NETTA (*Overlapping above*): Olive had no way of knowing Buddy'd be asking for those slippers.

BUDDY (*Overlapping*): It's O.K., it doesn't matter. Good Lord.

OLIVE: If they're so important, then they're still around. Now, there's coffee on the stove.

NETTA: There's going to be no shortage of coffee for you.

OLIVE: And there's sugar.

ELDON: They've saved up their stamps for a month.

NETTA: Eldon, we've done nothing of the kind.

ELDON: We've killed the fatted calf.

NETTA: We've killed the fatted goose and I'm not joking; I've never seen so much grease in my life.

BUDDY: Coffee sounds good. I heard the Italians made such great coffee. Wooee! I had to spit it out on the ground. Tasted like they'd burned it.

ELDON: You won't spit this out.

(BUDDY *and* OLIVE *exit*)

NETTA: Buddy, don't get in Nora's way out there. (*Sotto voce*) She's about out of patience with Olive. Are those your dad's records?

ELDON: I'll say one thing, he's made it fun figuring out what he's been up to in there. Everything's in code and symbols and God knows what.

NETTA: He always did keep things pretty close to his chest.

ELDON: I love it; it's not like figuring someone's books, it's like doing a puzzle. I swear, if Dad went into town to buy a bottle of Coca-Cola, he'd write in the ledger: "One B CC, five cents."

NETTA: You'll just have to ask him what some of—

ELDON: And spoil the fun? Not on your life.

NETTA: We don't know how much time—

ELDON: Besides, every time I ask him about anything, he goes senile on me. That's his new trick. Do you remember a Carl Saper? (NETTA *shakes her head*) Lottie?

LOTTIE: Let me in there, I'll burn the office and its contents.

ELDON: You ever heard of him?

LOTTIE: Just be sure you keep that door locked.

NETTA: Well, not to keep you out.

LOTTIE: That's right, you ask Olive what that means, she's probably got it all worked out.

NETTA: I'm sure nothing as piddlin' as a Yale padlock ever kept that one out of—well, nobody wants to hear mother-in-law talk. But yesterday she—

OLIVE (*Entering*): Mother!

NETTA (*Jumps a foot*): Oh, Olive! Scare me out of ten years' growth.

OLIVE: Did Granddaddy come through here?

ELDON: No, ma'am, we've been allowed to get something done without his supervision this afternoon.

OLIVE: I went in to see if he wanted to come to supper tonight; he isn't there. He isn't strong enough to go upstairs, is he?

NETTA: I looked in after dinner and he was dressed and sitting up. Told me to get out, so I got.

LOTTIE: He's come back to life out of contrariness.

OLIVE: Granddaddy?

NETTA: Lottie. (*Going off, calling*) Mr. Talley?

BUDDY (*Entering*): He's not around to the side.

NETTA (*Off*): Well, this is absurd. Mr. Talley?

OLIVE: Dad, did you park the Packard in the drive when you came back from town?

ELDON: I took the pickup.

OLIVE: Well, where'd you leave the Packard?

ELDON: Same place I always—

OLIVE: 'Cause unless someone's moved it, I can't see it out there.

ELDON: It's right in front of the pickup.

OLIVE: Well, I'm sorry, but it isn't.

ELDON: Well now, blue eyes; don't fly off crazy. Emmet's probably washing it around behind the barn.

OLIVE: Emmet Young is sitting on his duff, like he always is, whittling a stick.

ELDON (*Yelling out the window*): Emmet! Emmet, come in here.

OLIVE: Someday somebody's gonna hold a stick-whittling contest; I'm gonna enter Emmet Young and make my fortune.

NETTA (*Enters*): Oh, good Lord, he couldn't have got up and taken that car off.

ELDON: He doesn't even know how to drive it; he doesn't know the shift.

NETTA: Maybe he's out to the barn to look at the horses.

ELDON: There's no insurance on that car with him drivin' it either.

BUDDY: There's not been a horse on the place since I was a kid.

NETTA: Tell him that, and tell him they don't skate down on the mill pond anymore.

ELDON: He remembers what he wants to. (EMMET *enters*) Emmet, have you seen Dad since dinner time?

EMMET: Not since this morning. I been down to the pump house.

ELDON: You hear the car drive off? You see it?

EMMET: I had that auxiliary pump goin', I wouldn'ta heard nothin'.

ELDON: Well, look around and see if you can see the Packard. Damn it all.

(EMMET *leaves*)

NETTA: I better call Cliffy. Good Lord.

BUDDY: Don't bother the sheriff. I'll take the pickup and go along the road. We'll catch him.

OLIVE: Dad can do that. Or Emmet can go. (*Chasing after him*) Buddy, we have to go up and look in on June. Well, then I'm coming along.

BUDDY: You're helping Nora cook supper, I thought. (*He exits*)

OLIVE: Buddy Talley, I swear. You just got home, honey. You're only on leave for seventy-two hours. Honey! (*Storms back to the kitchen*)

NETTA: She's going right back to that kitchen. Nora's going to flat quit on us.

(*Everyone has left except* ELDON *and* LOTTIE)

ELDON: I knew Dad was half senile, but I— (*Pause. He notices that* LOTTIE *is standing frozen, doubled over in pain*) Are you in pain? (*Pause*) I wish you'd let the others know you're sick. (*Pause*) I wouldn't think it would be so painful. (*Pause*) Is there . . . ? (*She shakes her head, catches her breath*) Is it passing?

LOTTIE (*Nods*): Oh damn.

ELDON: Better?

LOTTIE (*Blissfully, breathlessly*): Oh! Gone! Gone completely. Blessed relief. Oh, wonderful. Oh, I'm walking on air. Nothing left of it at all.

ELDON: I wouldn't think it'd hurt so much.

LOTTIE: Oh, who knows anything about it. Oh my, I feel lovely. Oh, wonderful! It certainly is taking its time, isn't it?

ELDON: Enough of that.

LOTTIE: It's only pain, after all.

ELDON: When do you go back to see the doctors?

LOTTIE: I think they've lost interest. All the girls have kicked the bucket except five of us. One of those is about to go, poor thing. The other four of us are holding out on them. The doctors'd like to close the books, publish their reports. We're

not going to let them. We're in a race to the . . . (*Laughing*)
Well, I was going to say to the bitter end. That's the damned
truth. (*Phone rings*) That's for me.

NETTA (*In the hall*): I got it, Lottie.

LOTTIE: I'll get it. You know better than that. (*Standing in
the hall, within sight*. NETTA *is out of sight*)

NETTA: Hello.

LOTTIE: Who is it? Is that for me?

NETTA: Would you just sit down, Lottie, everything isn't for
you. It's Cliffy.

LOTTIE: What's the sheriff doing calling here? Let me talk to
him.

ELDON: Is Dad all right?

NETTA: Well, is he all right? We've been worried sick.

LOTTIE: I don't want you tying up the telephone here tonight.

NETTA: He's all right. They're bringing him back. Harley is.
What say?

ELDON: You're quick enough when the phone rings.

LOTTIE: If that's my one pleasure, I don't want it denied me.

ELDON: Who's the secret admirer?

LOTTIE: I have my enjoyments.

ELDON: Lottie, with all those long-distance calls all winter, I hope you haven't been talking to that Friedman character, trying to plead Sally's case.

NETTA: We appreciate it.

LOTTIE: Eldon Talley, I don't know what you're talking about.

NETTA: Goodbye now. He's all right.

ELDON: What happened?

NETTA: I don't know, Eldon. Cliffy says they're driving him back. (*Exits*)

LOTTIE: With Olive sprucing up the parlor for a funeral, the least Dad could do is oblige everybody by dying.

ELDON: I don't want to hear that, Lottie. We just count our blessings and go on with what has to be done.

LOTTIE: What are you so feisty about tonight?

ELDON: Nothing at all. Maybe I'm excited about Timmy coming home, having Buddy here. Work agrees with me. I guess I'm not the martyr you are.

LOTTIE: Me? Shit. If that clock company hadn't gone out of business, I'd have sued them for every dime they had. Made a bundle. When did ol' Marie Curie kick the bucket? Ten years ago, bless her, or I'd sue her, too. 'Course, ol' Marie didn't tell us to point the brushes with our tongues.

ELDON: Oh, come on.

LOTTIE: Give you the willies? Every one of us did it. Had a little pot of radium paint to paint the clock dials with. Point the brush on our tongues, dip it in the little pot of radium paint, paint a number, point the brush on our little tongues.

ELDON: Come on, now, just shut up about it.

LOTTIE: What did we know about radium poisoning? The foreman told us not to. Thought it was unsanitary. Gave us little
sponges for the purpose. Only one girl used it that I know of.
Didn't like the taste. Hell, I couldn't tell it had any. 'Course,
she went, too—poor baby. Cancer of the bone.

ELDON: Oh, God.

LOTTIE: Well, Eldon, that's the rewards of a delicate palate.
(OLIVE *runs to front door and out.* TIMMY *follows her*)

NETTA (*Entering*): They're pulling up out front. Harley brought
him back.

ELDON: Where the devil had he got to?

NETTA: He did, he took the Packard. Harley's driving him
back in it. (*She exits again*)

BUDDY (*Entering*): Harley's got him. Looks like he's OK; they're
bringing him in. You never saw anything like it.

NETTA (*Off*): Come on, back up, here we go.

OLIVE (*Off*): Upsy-daisy!

HARLEY (*Off*): I tell you, he is a cuss!

TALLEY (*Off*): Wooo! Oh boy.

HARLEY: Wooo, I bet! You shoulda seen it. I was—(*Entering
with* TALLEY, NETTA, *and* OLIVE)—just driving by; I saw the
car had run into a ditch up at the hill. I thought—

ELDON: Is he all right?

HARLEY: —What the hell's going on—excuse me, Netta. Oh, he's fine. Old man Talley's got more guts than an army mule. Ain't ya?

TALLEY: Who? Who?

HARLEY: He's been sayin' that all the way. I parked my car, got out, and there he was up on the hill—dressed for the dead of winter, standing in the middle of the graveyard. Caretaker— (NETTA *and* OLIVE *say,* "Oh, my Lord," "Oh no")—said he'd been taking up one spot and looking around, then moving to another spot. Admiring the sunset, I guess.

BUDDY: Selecting his site, maybe.

NETTA: Oh, his place is all laid out.

ELDON: He's right by Momma.

TALLEY: Who? Say who?

NETTA: He's overexcited.

OLIVE: You don't want to stay here, Granddaddy. You want to go into your room?

TALLEY: Here, you! Blamed woman. Let me be. Who? Say who?

NETTA: What, Mr. Talley?

TALLEY: Who?

HARLEY: Sounds like a goddamned owl.

NETTA: Harley, don't be disrespectful. This is still Mr. Talley's house.

TALLEY: Blamed woman, Get her off me.

ELDON: He's not hurt none.

OLIVE: I've never seen him so rambunctious.

HARLEY: Shoot no, try to hurt him.

TALLEY: Who?

ELDON: What kind of shape is the car in?

NETTA: He doesn't hear. Mr. Talley, you want to go? You want to go to your room?

HARLEY: It drives good. That's the miracle. I don't think he knows where the brake is on it.

OLIVE: Granddaddy? You want to go?

TALLEY: Blamed woman.

ELDON: He doesn't know how to drive it at all; he doesn't know the shift.

HARLEY: Run it into a ditch to stop it; might be scratched up.

(ELDON *exits*)

NETTA: The important thing is, he's not hurt.

HARLEY: Son-of-a-gun, you opened up the parlor. They're really putting on the dog for you.

TALLEY: Fine room.

HARLEY: Yes, sir, beautiful room.

TALLEY: Fine room. Chair. Chair.

NETTA: Help him to his chair, Buddy.

OLIVE: Here you go, Granddaddy.

TALLEY: Get me to sit down. What? Who?

NETTA: This morning he was sharp as a tack. He went into his office.

HARLEY: It's good to see old Buddy, isn't it? All dressed up like a soldier. I thought you'd be in civvies for one day at least.

OLIVE: You're always in the service, Harley. You know that.

HARLEY: I didn't know I was gonna be impressed or I'd have prepared myself.

OLIVE: Uncle Sam may need you at any time, night or day.

BUDDY: And he ain't the only one.

TALLEY: Who? Oh boy. (*Smiles, grunts*) Oh boy. (*Smiles, grunts*) Oh boy.

NETTA: What's that, Mr. Talley? Oh no. No, Papa, not here. Oh dear, Olive, help me get him into the bathroom— Oh, Mr. Talley. Oh no.

HARLEY: Wooooee! Oh boy, for sure.

BUDDY: Well, Momma said, "It's his house."

HARLEY: Netta, you said, "Do you want to go?" and he went.

OLIVE: Both of you, now.

NETTA: Don't you laugh.

HARLEY: Never in my life seen a man so pleased with himself.

NETTA (*She and* OLIVE *have moved* TALLEY *to the door. They stop*) Mr. Talley? No? Well, come on. Wait. Don't you laugh, you'll be like this someday. I think that was a false alarm. Do you want to go to the bathroom?

TALLEY: Chair.

NETTA: He's fine. He's been gassy is all. Don't you laugh.

ELDON (*Entering*): Whole side of the car is scratched from front to back.

NETTA: Don't you want to take off your coat?

OLIVE: Are you too warm?

TALLEY: Who?

NETTA: What does he think I'm saying?

OLIVE: Aren't you too warm?

HARLEY: I haven't seen a coat of that quality in twenty years.

NETTA: Oh, he was always a dresser.

OLIVE: Weren't you, Mr. Talley?

TALLEY: Hey, hey. Let me go! Blamed. Blamed.

(OLIVE *has got* MR. TALLEY'S *overcoat off him*)

BUDDY: Look at that suit material.

OLIVE: Well, it wouldn't hurt you to have one good suit. When you own the garment factory in town, you might as well dress like it.

HARLEY: Shoot—nothing like this ever came out of Lebanon. One hundred percent cashmere, made by hand in Boston. Him and Dad both thought they were hot stuff. Only good it did Dad was give him something fancy to be buried in.

NETTA: It isn't just show.

HARLEY: Wait till you see me tonight. I'm gonna put on the dog for you.

OLIVE: Everybody's gonna look their best tonight.

ELDON: That's the nicest bonus of having the boys back—the girls all show them a little leg.

OLIVE: Dad.

ELDON: You wouldn't know it to look at her tonight, but Olive is often as not in men's trousers when you're not here.

BUDDY: She's wearing what?

OLIVE: They're slacks and you're never gonna see me in them.

BUDDY: Good.

ELDON: That's one thing we're not gonna manufacture down at that plant.

HARLEY: No, sir.

BUDDY: Shorts and halters maybe.

ELDON: Now that's something we might consider.

OLIVE: Nobody in this town would wear those, I hope.

BUDDY: Oh, I could name a couple.

ELDON: I bet you could.

TALLEY: Who?

BUDDY: Olive, I thought you aired out the room, I swear it still has a smell.

(HARLEY *whispers something to* ELDON)

NETTA: Now! You. That's the coal furnace; the room's been closed up since last winter.

ELDON: I remember when I was a boy, we heated with wood. The whole house when you came into it had that wonderful smell of wood smoke. I always—

TALLEY: No, sir.

ELDON: What say, Dad? I think he's calming down.

TALLEY: Said coal. This house was fired by a coal furnace. Bought and paid for it myself. School was coal, church was coal, City Hall was coal. Me and Elijah Scott bought a half interest in the delivery service. Talley place got a new furnace, everybody in town had to have one.

ELDON: Well then, what am I remembering?

TALLEY: You're remembering laying with one of your floozies out in her daddy's smokehouse.

LOTTIE: Yes, he's calmed down to normal.

HARLEY: I think.

TALLEY: You're thinking of some roadhouse speakeasy. Contracted for the school delivery, contracted for the Municipal Building . . . Me and my brother, Whistler, gave that river land for a park to the city. Gave it free and clear.

HARLEY: Yes, sir, and you've had the whole town by the gonads ever since.

TALLEY: Yes, sir. Knew it at the time. So did they. Sit down, Mr. Campbell. I can't look up.

HARLEY: Yes, sir. That old boy used to scare the tar outta me.

BUDDY: I love him. General Clark put me on a plane to get me back for Granddad's funeral; I get here and look at him—ornery as an ox.

ELDON: We just count our blessings, Buddy, and go on with what has to be done.

HARLEY: Hey, I saw that Jew's dilapidated old Plymouth.

ELDON: The hell you say.

HARLEY: Parked down the way.

ELDON: If I thought he was still on the property, I'd go out hunting.

HARLEY: Looks like he'd run outta gas, pushed it off the road.

BUDDY: Don't get excited, Aunt Lottie, he's long gone now.

LOTTIE: I'm sure he is, thanks to you.

HARLEY: So that's Sally's new beau.

BUDDY: Yeah, isn't he a prize?

HARLEY: She sure can pick 'em.

LOTTIE: You two, I'm gonna get out that broom.

HARLEY: Listen, I got to go to the draft board yet; this stop wasn't on my schedule. I still haven't had a chance to go home and change my clothes, wash up.

NETTA: You look fine.

HARLEY: No, I said. A big dinner like you got planned, Mary Jo would have a conniption if we didn't dress up and turn out.

ELDON: I'm not used to these fancy late-supper parties.

NETTA: Not with the family, anyway.

BUDDY: That's right, Dad. I'm about starved.

HARLEY (*Sotto voce*): Occasion like this, might break out some of that old Prohibition stump water you used to run.

ELDON: Come on now, what the old man don't know won't hurt him. That was in my greener years.

HARLEY: I remember it had a pretty potent kick.

ELDON: Not at all, now, not at all. Sometimes we let that age ten or fifteen minutes.

OLIVE: The women didn't hear that.

HARLEY: So, you guys had a chance to talk about that Delaware Industries offer? You read those brochures I left you?

BUDDY: I looked at the pictures.

ELDON: He was just telling me how he didn't know anything about it.

BUDDY: Only what you wrote me, Dad, that's what I know. And what Mom was tellin' me out in the kitchen.

NETTA: Buddy, now. No factory talk, and none tonight, or the women will just leave you sitting at the table.

HARLEY: I think it's beautiful. 'Course I don't know the first thing about it, to hear Eldon.

BUDDY: I'm always willing to listen.

OLIVE: She's not joking now.

HARLEY: O.K., O.K. (*Lighting a cigarette, gives* BUDDY *one*)

OLIVE: Harley Campbell and Kenneth Talley! You two, if you want to smoke a cigarette, you step outside or into another room. Mother'll have your hide.

HARLEY: Son-of-a-gun, I clean forgot.

OLIVE: Oh, I'm sure. I'm not kidding now!

HARLEY: I know, I know. What a bossy woman. Come on. I don't know how you put up with her.

BUDDY: Oh, I need it. Keeps me in step.

(OLIVE *chases them out the French doors*)

OLIVE: You can't tell me Mary Jo allows you to smoke in the parlor, I don't care how modern you are.

(LOTTIE *lights a cigarette,* OLIVE *exits*)

NETTA: She's going right back to that kitchen. She's already put so much spice in that pie, the devil himself couldn't eat it.

ELDON: That was a pretty clever maneuver to get Buddy outside. What's he telling him out there?

NETTA: Eldon, I'd like it to be peaceful this evening. Nothing can be decided till Timmy gets home, anyway.

ELDON: I know that. Tell Buddy. Tell Harley.

NETTA: You can all talk on Thursday. I don't want you and Buddy in an argument. (*She exits*)

ELDON: I know.

TALLEY: All gone. All gone. You. Sally. Answer up when you're spoke to.

ELDON: That's Lottie, Dad.

TALLEY: We all of us got to go, young lady. You scared of going?

LOTTIE: Well, I'm hoping not to see you there, Daddy, wherever it is. (*She looks to* ELDON)

ELDON: I didn't say anything.

TALLEY: I ain't. Ain't anxious; ain't scared. I've lived a good, clean, Christian life.

Farley Granger and Edward Seamon

Farley Granger and Robert MacNaughton

Farley Granger and Joyce Reehling Christopher

Julie Bargeron, Steve Decker and Edward Seamon

Farley Granger and Helen Stenborg

LOTTIE: If there's a heaven, Daddy, you'll burn in hell.

ELDON: That's not called for.

TALLEY: Charlotte Talley, besides painting numbers on fifty-cent watches, what have you done? Run off to be independent, come hangdoggin' it back ten years later—

LOTTIE: Thirteen. And if there'd been another place to go—

ELDON: She got sick, Dad.

TALLEY: Stood right here on this carpet with her college certificate in her hand and called me a curmudgeon. Said she was going off to work among the poor people. Didn't like being rich. Ended up painting clock faces in a factory in Connecticut. That place closed down and where did she go? Speak up. Chicago. Working in some socialist outfit. Trying to teach something to the colored kids. Guess they couldn't stomach her either, 'cause the first thing you know, here she comes back again.

LOTTIE: I stayed in Chicago until I got too weak to work. And it's the only time I've been of any use to anybody.

TALLEY: And what you got to show for it?

LOTTIE: More than you could imagine.

TALLEY: Come hangdoggin' it back, looking for the curmudgeon to feed you. Fine family I raised; fine children, the two of you.

LOTTIE: I'm not going to have a conversation with you, Daddy; I choose the people I talk to.

TALLEY: Comes a time in a man's life he totals it all up; adds it all up. I go and the place goes to blazes.

ELDON: We'll just have to do the best we can. (*Low*) If we ever get the chance.

LOTTIE: Amen. He's not afraid of going because he doesn't think he will.

ELDON: He may not, Lottie, he may not. He's never made a will . . . He's used a different lawyer for every transaction. Did you know he owns half the Bassett farm?

LOTTIE: He's probably got something on Leslie Bassett, the poor bugger.

TALLEY: Place has gone to the devil.

ELDON: The Bassett farm? Did Leslie take out a mortgage from you?

TALLEY: Talley place, I say. Wouldn't invite a dog in here. All going to the devil without me.

ELDON: Dad, with the war on, everything is run down. (*Low, where Talley can't hear*) And you are still very much with us.

TALLEY: Yes, I am, sir, and you'll learn to respect the fact. If Stuart had lived, you'da seen something.

LOTTIE: Oh boy.

ELDON: Just don't start that, Dad.

TALLEY: Day Stuart was born I changed that factory name to Talley & Son. It wasn't named for you, I can tell you.

ELDON: I know. And from the day Stuart died you never set foot in the place.

TALLEY: Look at you with that ledger. You go in that office, all those papers, you know what you'd do? You'd alphabetize them.

ELDON: Well, that's more than you've done. What does that signify? Can't even read it. Carl Saper, December 1913. (TALLEY *laughs*) What's funny? Is he laughing or crying?

TALLEY: Well, sir. Old Carl Saper had thirty acres' wild land. Had eighty-five black-walnut trees on it. Wasn't worth nothin'.

LOTTIE: But you took it away from him anyway, didn't you, Daddy?

TALLEY: No, lady.

LOTTIE: From Carl and Ruth both.

TALLEY: No, sir. Loaned him a bundle, mortgaged the land. Nine thousand dollars, fifteen years. Dern fool tried to raise geese. Didn't know the first thing about it. Feathers everywhere. Said he couldn't pay that year. Couldn't pay the interest, couldn't pay the principal; said, "Don't take the land away, leave the land in my name and take the walnuts for payment. Black walnuts sellin' for forty cents a gunnysack, hulled." Well, sir, I went down there, looked the place over, said, "Next year you pay, this year what I can make off that thirty acres of bottom land is mine." Wrote it out, notarized by Norma Ann Comstock. Had the colored boys from Old Town pick up the walnuts, haul 'em to the exchange. Called a company in Minneapolis, Minnesota; they came here, cut down the walnut trees for fancy lumber to make veneer out of 'em. I made eleven thousand dollars off that no-count wild land in 19 and 13. Told old Saper, now you got good pastureland. I should charge you for clearing it. Fool tried to sue me. Hadn't read the paper. Read what you sign, I told him. Use your eyes. Know the worth of a thing. (*He laughs*)

LOTTIE (*Without looking up*): Is he laughing or crying?

ELDON: Just when you think his mind is gone, it's back.

TALLEY: Dern fool sold at loss not to sell to the Talleys. See what's happening and happen first.

LOTTIE and ELDON (*With* TALLEY): . . . happen first.

TALLEY: Eldon never looked up from his bookkeeping. Start keeping books, you end up keeping books.

ELDON: I don't keep books, sir. I have a girl who does that for me, and she has an assistant now.

TALLEY: Only thing you ever did on your own was run whiskey to St. Louis during Prohibition.

ELDON: You'll find I've done a little better lately. My factory is worth double what your bank is.

TALLEY: Thought I didn't know how you was enhancing the Talley name with your whores.

ELDON: I don't spend half the week at church shaking hands with all my neighbors and the other half at the bank foreclosing on their mortgages, no. My factory is putting out the best quality pair of army fatigues made anywhere, no thanks to you, and after the war Timmy and I intend—

TALLEY: Fine children. Get me up. Up.

ELDON: All right. Don't listen; you never did.

TALLEY: Won't have it. Fine children. Up. Up. Get me to my room, blamed. Blamed.

ELDON (*Over*): Here, don't go alone; wait and I'll help you.

VIOLA (*Entering*): Excuse me, Mr. Eldon. Everybody was around to the kitchen, so I came to the front.

TALLEY: If you had any gumption, you'd tell those Delaware boys to soak their heads. Got no gumption.

ELDON: I did, thank you, and it's no business of yours.

VIOLA: I knocked, I couldn't get nobody to hear. I didn't want to wake up the baby again.

LOTTIE: Come on into the room.

TALLEY: Who?

VIOLA: Mr. Eldon, could I have a minute of your time?

ELDON (*Moving* TALLEY *to the door*): I can't talk now.

VIOLA: This is important to you, Mr. Eldon.

TALLEY: Me and Elijah Scott got a furnace; everybody in town had to have one . . .

VIOLA: Eldon. (*Pause*) If I could just—talk to you a minute.

ELDON: Not right now, Viola. This isn't a good time. Or place.

TALLEY: Who's here?

VIOLA: I gotta tell you something.

ELDON: Fine, come to the factory on Friday or next Monday, talk to Mrs. Willy. (*He and* TALLEY *leave*)

VIOLA: Well . . . I guess I been put in my place. The Talleys was always good at that.

LOTTIE: Sit down, Viola, before you fall.

VIOLA: I walked from the house; one of the boys took the truck. Is that Mr. Eldon's boy out there with Mr. Campbell?

LOTTIE: Yes, that's Kenneth. Worked at Dad's bank before the war.

VIOLA: Shoot, when was I ever in your bank? He looks good in his uniform. The young 'un's a sailor, ain't he?

LOTTIE: Timmy's in the Marines; out in the Pacific. He'll be back day after tomorrow.

VIOLA: I remember Timmy from the garment factory. All them sailors over fighting in their white uniforms. I wouldn't want to do their laundry.

LOTTIE: I don't imagine.

VIOLA (*Sighs, sits*): No, Miss Charlotte. I tell you, I'm plum might worn frazzled this evening. I didn't get no sleep. I was up with the twins.

LOTTIE: Twins? I don't remember you having twins.

VIOLA: Oh, Lord help me, that's all I'd need. Mrs. Niewonker's two. I'm taking care of them while she's at the hospital having another one. Avalaine didn't come home and I couldn't get my boys to help.

LOTTIE: That's not men's work, I know.

VIOLA: Hell, ain't nothin' men's work to hear them tell it. Avie's the worker. Just last month she and me washed down the whole Farley house. 'Course now she's run off.

LOTTIE: Avalaine ran off? Where to?

VIOLA: Who with is more like it. Who knows. She just took off, off and took. Seventeen years old, looks like twenty-five. She was hanging down to the roll arena and around the Blue Line.

LOTTIE: What the hell is the Blue Line?

VIOLA: Roadhouse. A mile outside of town.

LOTTIE: Well, if you're worried, you want me to call Cliffy for you?

VIOLA: Oh hell, Lottie. I told her to go. I said, you fly away on. Fly away on. There ain't nothin' here. Don't talk to me about opportunity. It's all the same. You're workin' for the Talleys or you're working for the Campbells or you're working for the Farleys. You fly away on and don't slow down to say I'm leavin'. (*Laughing*) And I guess she didn't.

LOTTIE: I guess not.

VIOLA: Can't blame 'em for doin' what you told 'em to do.

HARLEY (*Entering with* BUDDY): It's clearing up. I swear this morning it looked like it was gonna rain like pourin' piss out of a boot. Oh, Lord, excuse me, ladies, I didn't know you was in here.

VIOLA (*Pause*): Well, none of that work is gonna finish itself.

HARLEY: Viola, I thought the service for Vaughan was very well handled.

VIOLA: Thank you, Mr. Campbell. I appreciate it. And thank you for coming by personally with the telegram. Mom appreciated it.

NETTA (*Entering*): Viola, did you need something else?

VIOLA: No, nothin', thank you.

LOTTIE: I'll tell Eldon.

VIOLA: No, don't trouble him about me. I'll come by the office like he said. I should've known not to come up to the house. All you have a nice evening, now.

LOTTIE: You, too, Mrs. Platt.

(VIOLA *exits*)

HARLEY: I was down at their place, you never seen people living in conditions like that; all the windows wide open to the outside; flies thick as freckles on a turkey's egg.

LOTTIE: You're a rich man, Harley. You ought to send them some screen wire if you're so concerned.

HARLEY: Old man Platt would have it sold and drunk up before nightfall. I was the one took the telegram to her mother, said her son was killed. None of 'em can read. I had to read it to them.

BUDDY: That ain't easy. Who was he?

LOTTIE: Viola's brother. Vaughan.

NETTA: Vaughan Robinson.

HARLEY: Older than you, worked at the garage. Used to pitch for the softball. Lord, I'll tell you, I'd rather be over there fighting than back here bringing the word.

BUDDY: It isn't anything you have to do.

HARLEY: No, I do. I figure if I'm on the draft board helping to send you all over there, then when the telegram comes, I'm the one who should bring it to the family. I don't know. I started doing it, now people expect it. I'd a whole lot rather be in the middle of it over there with you.

BUDDY: I'm not in the middle of it. From what I read in the paper, says France is the middle of it.

HARLEY: We were all watching Anzio this winter, I can tell you. That didn't sound any too good.

BUDDY: Yeah, got pretty cold. We hadn't expected that.

NETTA: We all thought it was going to be another Corregidor.

BUDDY: No, no, it rained, there was a lot of mud. Did you worry about me, Aunt Lottie?

LOTTIE: Yes. I still do.

BUDDY: Well, don't.

NETTA: There's no hope of getting anything out of Buddy. Timmy's letters are full of the jungle and what everything is like. All we get out of Buddy is, "Well, there's not much to write."

(ELDON *enters*)

BUDDY: It's darn boring most of the time. Harley ought to be glad he's here with something to do.

NETTA: The washerwoman was just here looking for you.

ELDON: From what we read, it sounded like the Krauts had you guys in some kind of pincer action about half the time—

BUDDY: No, no, 'course it's a heck of a lot different from what it looks like from home. Half those guys Harley's so hot to join over there are gonna be killed and the other half would go AWOL if they had the chance. (TIMMY *enters*) So how's business on the home front, Dad? Harley says we're still making a killing down there.

ELDON: I don't know if you could say that.

HARLEY: Hell, we don't even sleep anymore. We're both of us down there twelve hours a day.

BUDDY: You still personally inspecting every pair of fatigues that goes out of the place?

ELDON: I am, yes, rejecting one out of five 'cause we've taken on more than we can handle.

TIMMY: Hey, Dad, you know what?

NETTA: Come on now, you can talk about this after supper.

ELDON: We're not going to talk about anything, honey, till Timmy gets home.

HARLEY: Hell, Timmy'll make enough off this deal to start up a shop of his own if he loves it so much.

ELDON: Well, that factory's more Timmy's concern than any of ours. I've always figured Buddy'd want the bank and the factory'd go to Timmy. As far as I'm concerned, Sally gets nothing unless she changes her tune.

BUDDY: Shoot, the sooner Sally just waltzes on out of here, the happier everybody will be.

HARLEY: Especially with the sort she's been hanging around with lately.

(LOTTIE *stomps out of the room*)

ELDON: I think the Talleys got to have one in every generation.

NETTA: You know how she is about Sally. She's tried to influence that girl since the day she was born.

HARLEY: Well, I'd like to include Timmy and everybody, too, but it's the Fourth of July and we got till the tenth. That's cutting it a bit close for comfort.

BUDDY: Who the heck is Delaware Industries, anyway. I never heard of them.

HARLEY: You know all their products.

ELDON: It doesn't matter, I tell you, it's not gonna happen.

HARLEY: You know everything they make. I can't think of one right off the bat.

ELDON: Country Oven Bread.

HARLEY: Country Oven Bread.

ELDON: Baked in Pittsburgh.

NETTA: Tastes like it, too.

HARLEY: They started out as an insurance company.

ELDON: That tells you right there how far they can be trusted.

HARLEY: Used to be in Delaware, now they've moved to Baton Rouge.

ELDON: That's interesting, too. Delaware Industries, Baton Rouge, Louisiana. Man said they had a company that baked bread, had a company that made coils for a car, owned natural gas in Kansas and Oklahoma. I said to the man, "It used to be a fellow was in the business of making something. When someone asks me what business I'm in, I say, As long as the war's on, Talley & Son is in the business of making army fatigues. What business do you say you're in?" And the man says, "Well, we're in the business of making money."

HARLEY: Nobody told me we didn't want to turn a profit down there.

ELDON: Harley, I love you like a son, but I'm not going to get into this argument with you.

BUDDY: I don't know what they want with us, anyway.

HARLEY: Well, see, they're starting reconversion plans for postwar production.

BUDDY: Whoa!

HARLEY: That may sound a little funny to a soldier.

BUDDY: No, heck, I see it, everybody's looking ahead; you'd be a fool not to.

ELDON: And, looking ahead, we put in an order, which was Timmy's idea by the way.

HARLEY: The timing maybe, who's to say whose idea it was?

TIMMY: Harley was dead set against it.

ELDON: Soon as the war is over, three hundred bolts of nylon will be coming to us every week.

BUDDY: I thought you couldn't get it.

HARLEY: The Du Ponts needed the money, if you can believe it, and we had it that day.

ELDON: If you can't buy the nylon, take over the company that has it, next best thing.

BUDDY: Heck, better.

HARLEY: Hell, yes; excuse me, Netta. We have them over a goddamn barrel.

BUDDY: Excuse him, Mom. Where did these jokers come from?

HARLEY: We've only been working for them for three years.

ELDON: As of last January, Harley's got us working their orders a hundred percent.

HARLEY: You think a jerkwater outfit like us could get a war contract?

ELDON: No, they got the executives, they got the lobby in Washington, they got the credit, they got the pull, and they got the contract! And they do not own a single darned sewing machine. Everything is subcontracted to a bunch of dummies like us.

HARLEY: But now they've got the government to build them a plant down in Louisiana so they can get the whole operation under one roof.

ELDON: Now if that's not slicker than snot on a doorknob, I don't know what is.

BUDDY: I'm sorry, Dad, I don't see your point.

HARLEY: He thinks they're going to take over his name and turn out crap.

ELDON: I do, yes; among other things, I do. And it may be old-fashioned to have pride in the product that has the name Talley & Son on it—

HARLEY: I can't make him understand they don't want his damned name either.

ELDON: I didn't build something up to have it torn down. And Timmy is expecting that factory to be there for him when he gets out, and it's gonna be there!

HARLEY: Eldon, I tell you I'm tired! I tell you when Dad shot himself, I went right from the graveyard to the factory without changing clothes and cut pants till after midnight, was back on the job at six the next morning—thirteen years ago, and I haven't let up yet. Didn't even have time to order a marker for Dad's grave. Now, it killed him, but it's not going to kill me.

(Pause)

ELDON: Maybe we all should take a month off after the war; start treating ourselves.

NETTA: There's a stone now.

ELDON: Honey.

HARLEY: What say?

NETTA: On your dad's grave.

HARLEY: Oh, I know. I went back five years later, somebody had put up a stone. Must have been Mom. Made for the both of them, her birth date already cut into it. She's all the time afraid someone might say they had to spend a nickel on her. Thinks we're still living in the Depression. I gotta go.

NETTA: She's a good—

TALLEY (*Entering*): Blame it, blame it.

OLIVE (*Trailing him*): Granddaddy, don't you want to lie down?

NETTA: What's he doing up?

OLIVE: He came through the kitchen. I thought he was trying to head back to the Packard.

BUDDY: Olive.

OLIVE: Well, is he all right?

TALLEY: Blamed woman. Stop houndin' me. Whole blamed family buzzing like a swarm of gnats in here.

HARLEY: Eldon, I didn't work any harder than you and Tim, but I'm about due for that vacation.

ELDON: You go with Delaware and you retire completely. They don't want any of us down there.

TALLEY: Buzz, buzz, buzz, buzz . . .

OLIVE: I thought they offered you and Harley and Buddy an executive job as—

ELDON: Boy, everybody in the family has to put in their two cents. They offered me and Harley and Timmy, and Buddy, I guess, if he wants it, a position on their board of directors or board of— What is it?

HARLEY: Advisory board.

ELDON: Which means our names in a list on their stationery. For what it's worth, Harley, that place has been my life. And it's going to be Timmy's life.

NETTA: Eldon.

ELDON: Well, honey, what else, except for my family, have I had?

NETTA: I wouldn't know.

BUDDY: They want to move the plant to Louisiana?

HARLEY: The machines sure, use the building here for a warehouse.

NETTA: What would happen to all the girls who work down there? Where would they go?

HARLEY: Oh, good Lord, Netta; they'd go to Louisiana. Hell, excuse me, damn it, they're—excuse me—riff-raff anyway.

Divorced women, unmarried mothers. The town would be better off without them.

NETTA: Now you're sounding like Mr. Talley.

HARLEY: Well, it's about time somebody did.

TALLEY: Never did care. Never did. No interest in that factory down there. Tell you why.

ELDON: Oh, Lord.

HARLEY: 'Cause you was having too much fun down at the bank.

TALLEY: Sir, when I'm talking.

HARLEY: Yes, sir.

TALLEY: Tell you why. Moral corruption. Never trusted those women. Broken homes and moral weakness. Just like others I could mention.

ELDON: But won't.

TALLEY: Sir, they're a bunch of no-goods making pants for another bunch of no-goods who are somewhere making shirts for the first no-goods. Scum of the earth.

ELDON: Right, Dad. You want to go to your room?

TALLEY: Harley, my boy, you'd do well, sir, to remember who the head of the Talley household is.

ELDON: You hear that? He's as lucid as a windowpane when he wants to be.

HARLEY: Boy, am I late for everything. Listen, I got to go to the draft-board people, I'm miles late.

BUDDY: They'll be closed by now.

HARLEY: Hell, the telegraph office doesn't close now till eleven.

NETTA: You be back here by eight and don't forget.

HARLEY: I'm gonna be busier than a cat with two tails till then, let me tell you.

BUDDY: I'll run you into town.

OLIVE: Buddy.

BUDDY: It'll only take five minutes to drop him at the Laclede Hotel and be back.

OLIVE: We have to check on June, remember?

BUDDY: The telegraph office still at the hotel building?

HARLEY: No, no, I'll borrow your pickup, if that's all right?

ELDON: Sure, take it.

BUDDY: No trouble.

OLIVE: Buddy!

BUDDY: June's all right. Oh. Maybe I'd better.

HARLEY: Yeah, you check up on little June and maybe talk about getting her a little brother.

ELDON: We'll thrash this out; you'll see the light. (*He walks* HARLEY *to the door*)

BUDDY: Honey, you want to come upstairs and check up on June? Maybe check up on Kenny, Jr., while we're at it.

OLIVE: Oh! You!

ELDON (*Returning*): Buddy, we're expecting your support in this.

BUDDY: Yes, sir. I know, sir. (*He and* OLIVE *exit*)

TALLEY: Old Whistler up there singing his songs.

NETTA: What's he talking about?

ELDON: The graveyard, I guess. Had an adventure, didn't you?

TALLEY: Yes, sir. Drove the Packard. Good driving car.

ELDON: Dad, do you think you can come into the office now. There's things we should go over.

TALLEY: Singing "*Una furtiva lagrima.*"

ELDON: Boy, you hear what you want to, don't you?

NETTA: Don't get him upset.

ELDON: Sure.

NETTA: Eldon, this business deal isn't more important than keeping peace in the family.

ELDON: I know.

(NETTA *exits*)

TIMMY: Dad?

ELDON: Dad?

TALLEY: Still going at it. Talkin' a blue streak.

TIMMY: Yes, sir, your brother Whistler was going a blue streak
and you were answering him right back. Caretaker thought
he had a madman on his hands, didn't he? (*To* ELDON) What
I want to tell you, sir—remember how you always said, "It
makes a difference when you do something right"? Well, what
I didn't know was everybody wasn't doing it the way we were.
I didn't know we were anything special. But then— (*To audience*) See, the Marines get real cocky about what they look
like—if you're on ship, you dress sharp. And they try to fit
you right on your first issue at least. But those fatigues leave
the factory about as stiff as a cardboard, so the guys all try to
break them down, soften them up; then they iron a crease in
them. So, once about a dozen of the guys tied their new
fatigues to a hook and dragged them along behind the ship for
about a week. They came out of that salt water soft as a chamois
cloth. Only most of them had shrunk about an inch. I told the
guys my dad's factory must of made the ones that hadn't shrunk
'cause we always shrink the material before we cut it. Dad,
you know what? They ironed them out, put them on, and in
the pocket of every good pair they found a little wadded-up
strip of paper that said "Inspected by E. Talley." I was real
popular, for about a week. (*To* ELDON) I knew you'd like to
hear that. But, Dad, I spent my whole life lookin' for things
that I knew you'd like. All the time I spent down at Talley &
Son, since I was eleven, was just so you'd notice me.

ELDON: Dad?

TIMMY: He really is asleep this time, he isn't just playing possum. (ELDON *goes into the office.* TIMMY *looks out the window*) Oh boy! Here comes trouble.

(AVALAINE PLATT *steps into the room*)

AVALAINE: Mr. Talley. Mr. Talley. Is Mr. Eldon in? (*Pause. She realizes he isn't going to speak. She walks to the front hall door, listens. There is a noise from the kitchen.* AVALAINE *goes past* TALLEY *to the back door and listens.* TIMMY *has gone*)

TALLEY: Whistler won't shut up. (AVALAINE *whirls around and looks at him*) Dead and buried, still won't quit yammering. (AVALAINE *looks around the room;* TALLEY *does not seem to know she is there. After a second she sits across the room from him, staring*) Old Whistler up there whistling, telling his tales. Can't hear yourself think.

AVALAINE: There you sit, you petrified old stick. You don't have a brain left in your evil old head, do you? You'd think the devil would come and collect his own before you became an embarrassment. Emmet said you was crazy half the time. I didn't believe it. (*Pause*) Who is it that's going to tell the mayor and the Town Hall how to run their business now? (*Pause*) I used to think you went stalking through Old Town at midnight, stealing babies to eat for breakfast. (*She stands*) You're just a dried-up old stick, ain't ya? (*She walks to him*) Ain't ya? Just a dried-up old horse. (*She tickles him on the ear*) Ain't ya? Huh?

(TALLEY *sits still for a moment. Then with one swift move he slaps her across the mouth, knocking her flat to the floor*)

TALLEY: There! Got ya! Ha!

AVALAINE: You son-of-a-bitch.

TALLEY: Get her out of here.

(*She yells in pain. From several places throughout the house people call, "What's going on?"* ELDON *opens the door from the office*)

ELDON: Jesus Christ!

NETTA (*Off*): What in the deuce is going on?

ELDON (*Overlapping*): Never mind, I'll take care of this. This isn't for you. (*Closes door*) You better go on down the road to your mother, Avalaine, she's looking for you.

AVALAINE: You think you got her and everybody else under your thumb, don't ya? Nobody dare say nothin'.

OLIVE (*Looking in*): Dad, what's going on?

ELDON: Just close that door there and never mind. (*She does.* TALLEY *goes into the office*) You just go on now, you can go across the fields.

(AVALAINE *holds her hand to her face. Her nose is bleeding*)

AVALAINE: That son-of-a-bitch broke my nose.

ELDON: I'm not going to call the sheriff, because you're going to go home now.

AVALAINE: Well, I'll tell you, Mr. Eldon, I've stayed with my mother's family for seventeen years; I got to thinkin' it's time I moved up here to live with my daddy.

ELDON: It wouldn't do for you to say anything againt the Talleys, Avalaine.

AVALAINE: You thought Ma wouldn't tell me about you and her.

ELDON: Whatever you've been told, there's nothing to tell. I'm surprised you'd believe lies like that.

(OLIVE *and* NETTA *open the doors*)

NETTA: I said, what's going on?

ELDON: Just stay out of here. (*He closes the doors*)

AVALAINE: As it happens, since Buddy Talley practically raped me last time he was home . . .

ELDON: I won't have you interfering with Buddy's life, and you're not going to interfere here with the Talleys.

AVALAINE: And since he come by the house to ask me to go into the woods with him last night, my ma thought it best to tell me as how Buddy Talley was my part-brother.

ELDON: That's not true, Avalaine, and I know your mother wouldn't say it.

AVALAINE: She thought she'd better let me know so's I don't conceive no two-headed bastards, both of us being your kids.

ELDON: I've heard all I'm listening to. You get out now.

AVALAINE: I tell you what, Papa. The Talleys are well treated in this town. I come up the hill to get my own. I figger you owe me my piece of all this.

ELDON: Avalaine Platt, the entire town knows you're a whore for sale to any buyer. Our own handyman, Emmet Young, has as much as told me—

AVALAINE: No more, no more, Papa, no more. I done what was necessary, but it ain't necessary no more, is it?

ELDON: You better go on down the hill, Avalaine. I'll talk with your mother. If you people are in trouble, maybe the Talleys can help. Now, you better just go back down the hill and I won't call Cliffy on you for breaking in the house.

AVALAINE: The window was wide open.

(HARLEY *opens the double doors*)

ELDON: Just stay out a minute—

HARLEY: Eldon—(*He can say no more. He carries a telegram, hardly sees* AVALAINE; *stands frozen a few feet inside the door, unable to speak*)

AVALAINE: You can call in the whole damn town as far as I'm concerned. I didn't steal nothing.

HARLEY: Eldon!

ELDON: Harley, we have a problem here, I'm trying to talk to someone right now.

HARLEY: Eldon, I'm sorry.

(*A long pause*)

ELDON: It's Timmy.

HARLEY: I'm sorry.

(OLIVE *opens the door.* NETTA *comes through bringing an ice bag.* OLIVE *and* BUDDY *enter the room.* LOTTIE *comes from upstairs.* TALLEY *enters from the office*)

OLIVE: Was she looking for her mother? What is that girl doing up here?

NETTA: I don't know what you're thinking, screaming at this child when she should have an ice pack on that face.

ELDON: Buddy, Olive. Not now.

NETTA: Eldon, I want to know why that girl isn't taken care of. She could have her nose broke.

OLIVE: Not now, Mother.

NETTA: What's the matter? Have I said something? Well, why are you looking at . . . What is it? Harley?

ELDON: It's all right, honey.

NETTA: Harley? (*Looking at* HARLEY. *He holds out the telegram*) That isn't true. That isn't true. (*Pause*) Harley . . . (*She takes a few uncertain steps toward* HARLEY *and faints, falling to the floor*)

Curtain

ACT II

Later that evening. LOTTIE, TIMMY, *and* ELDON *are in the dark living room. The only light comes from the hall.*

NETTA (*Off from upstairs*): I don't know why you say I fainted. I didn't faint.

OLIVE (*Off*): It doesn't matter, Mother.

NETTA (*Off*): Olive, please don't call me that.

OLIVE (*Off*): I know, I'm sorry. Should you be up?

NETTA (*Appearing in the hallway*): I'm fine. I can't just lay there.

OLIVE (*In hallway*): You rested some. You had a little nap.

NETTA: I didn't go to sleep. I couldn't sleep now. How could I sleep? (*She exits to the kitchen.* BUDDY *enters from the front door*)

OLIVE: Buddy, did you get Nora home O.K.?

BUDDY: Yeah. (ELDON *comes from the dark living room into the doorway, a letter in his hand*) What's that?

ELDON: Oh—I've been reading Timmy's—have you read this?

BUDDY: I didn't get a chance to see the ones that came yesterday.

ELDON: Listen—"Last night we spent on the deck of the transport bobbing up and down about a mile off two islands that are part of the Marianas. The big one is just another tangle of jungle and mangos, with all these razorback ridges running down it like the Arkansas backhills, only more so."

TIMMY: That's Saipan.

ELDON: "The little one is the first real farm island we've come across. It looks like a five-by-ten-mile Missouri."

TIMMY: That's Tinian. I took one look at Tinian and I thought I'd been witched. I thought I was home. I thought I'd woke up in the middle of the night and was looking out the back window of my room into Leslie Bassett's farm.

ELDON: "They just floated a flat chunk of Leclede County out to sea and tied it up in the Marianas."

OLIVE: Maybe you ought not to read that now, Dad.

ELDON: I was trying to get to this part. You remember what a baseball nut he was.

OLIVE (*To* BUDDY): Come on, honey, you're just going to get yourself upset. (*She exits to kitchen*)

BUDDY: In a sec'; I'm fine. What?

ELDON (*Reading*): "These islands are supposed to be a cake-walk. Ha. Ha. They said that about Tarawa. There's three big islands in the Marianas that are important to us and it looks like we'll be taking them on in order: short to second to first."

TIMMY: Saipan to Tinian to Guam.

ELDON: "Tinker to Evers to Chance . . ."

TIMMY: When we got the word we were going to the Marianas, some dog-face lieutenant said, "Marianas—shit, they sound like they was named after some Nip's Wop whore." We told him that the Spanish Jesuits named them for Queen Mariana, and the Jesuits were a tough band to tangle with. Boy, he was pissed beyond all proportion. It's amazing the pride some people take in their ignorance. 'Course he was already re-naming them the Eleanors. We told him Mrs. Roosevelt wouldn't want 'em after we got through, but he was all sozzled on patriotism. Well, half patriotism, half this cache of Nip beer, which, considering the Nips made it, is a hell of a lot better than Sterno and lemon extract, let me tell you.

(ELDON *goes out. He gives* BUDDY *the letter*)

BUDDY (*Reading*): "This shouldn't be bad, I'll let you know. We just got the call to hit the landing boats, so I'd better close. Tell Buddy, before he makes Rome, I'll be in Tokyo. Sorry about my handwriting, I'm writing this standing in line. Hurry up and wait."

TIMMY (*With* BUDDY): Hurry up and wait.

OLIVE (*Entering from the kitchen*): Buddy, don't hang around here in the dark, honey.

BUDDY: I'm not.

OLIVE: Where's Dad?

BUDDY: He went outside.

(*They move into the dark living room*)

OLIVE: Buddy, I can't take it here. We have to get a place of our own, a place in town.

BUDDY: I know; we will.

OLIVE: I never had a mother and dad that I remember. I thought this would be my family, but you see what it's like.

BUDDY: I know. Soon as I'm back. Not now.

OLIVE: Honey, we can't even talk.

BUDDY: I know.

OLIVE: The prices are just going to keep climbing. We might as well do it now as some other time.

BUDDY: I know. When I come home.

OLIVE: Honey, I know it's terrible to talk about it now, but you never answer any questions I write you.

BUDDY: I get them so long after you write . . .

OLIVE: Would you agree to a place if I find one? We can't have a minute to ourselves here.

NETTA (*Entering*): Don't stand in the dark, you two.

BUDDY: Are you all right, Mom?

NETTA: I wish everyone would quit asking me that. I have never blacked out in my life. For some reason I thought there was a chair right behind me. I know there isn't a chair there, but I thought there was and I put my hand back to steady myself, and there wasn't a chair there and I went over. I certainly fell down, but I didn't faint. I've never fainted in my life. Come on back into the kitchen with me and Harley. Don't hang around in here by yourselves. Where's your father?

BUDDY: He went out front.

NETTA: He's taking this very hard. Oh, Lord. Olive, I know, but don't let Eldon see you crying. And don't say anything, or—I don't know. I don't know. (*She goes out the front door*)

OLIVE: Said she didn't faint. Her eyes rolled back in her head, and she went down like a sack of potatoes.

BUDDY: Olive, good Lord.

OLIVE: I'm sorry, it's just—(BUDDY *starts for the kitchen*) Buddy, honey?

BUDDY: Come on into the light. Harley's in the kitchen all by himself.

OLIVE: Mother'll come back—and Dad.

BUDDY: Come on into the light. (*He goes. After a moment* OLIVE *follows*)

TIMMY: Nora, the cook, who used to be about my favorite person in the family, got so upset when they told her about me that she couldn't finish cooking supper. Buddy had to drive her home. They didn't have any vegetables at all. It's a good thing Olive made that pie.

ELDON (*Coming from the front with* NETTA): I don't want anything said in front of Dad.

NETTA: I know.

ELDON: If we ever got him to understand what had happened, it'd probably kill him.

NETTA: I know.

ELDON: Those two grandsons mean more to him than almost anything. Aren't you eating?

NETTA: I don't want anything, no. I'm fine. Eldon, come into the parlor now. You want to listen to the radio while Olive and I clean up.

ELDON: I don't know that I do; I have to get some air, the house is stifling. (*He steps back outside. After a moment she returns to the kitchen*)

TIMMY: Mom said Dad is taking this really hard, and he is. He went out to the barn and leaned up against the cattle stanchions and cried like I've never seen. 'Course when I was eight years old I went running out of the house, ran into that same room, leaned up against that same stanchion when my hamster died. And Dad came and found me there, so he maybe was remembering that, too.

NETTA (*Entering with* HARLEY, BUDDY, *and* OLIVE): Just see if he doesn't want to come in with us.

BUDDY: The sky cleared up.

HARLEY: There's even going to be a moon.

BUDDY: It's hot, but it's a beautiful night.

NETTA: I know, but he shouldn't be out there alone, brooding. (HARLEY *and* BUDDY *go out*)

NETTA: I don't know what to do for him.

OLIVE: I know.

NETTA: I just don't think he should be alone out there; he's not resilient like we are.

OLIVE: I know.

NETTA: He's got no bounce. I don't know what to say. I can't think of a thing to do for him.

OLIVE: I know, Netta.

NETTA: I don't know.

OLIVE: I know.

NETTA: I don't know.

OLIVE (*Turns the lights on*): Oh, my God, Aunt Lottie. Scare me to death. Sitting in here in the dark. Are you all right?

LOTTIE: Yes.

OLIVE: You should come into the kitchen and have something to eat.

LOTTIE: No.

NETTA: Has Sally come back to the house?

LOTTIE: No.

NETTA: She hasn't eaten a bite. I called her out back.

OLIVE: Maybe she went into town.

NETTA: Oh, Lord, I hope she doesn't hear from somebody in town!

LOTTIE: She'll be in soon.

NETTA: I know she's willful, but she's so strong and she sees so much at the army hospital. I just wish she was here. What were you doing in here by yourself?

LOTTIE: Nothing. (*She exits*)

HARLEY (*Entering from outside with* BUDDY *and* ELDON): I better call Mary Jo again, if I can use your phone.

NETTA: Sure, Harley, tell her we're fine. Now, there's a pie that Olive's made and there's coffee yet.

ELDON: Later on maybe.

HARLEY (*On phone*): Three-eight-O, please.

BUDDY: You bring it in, in a bit.

OLIVE: We will not, you'll come out and eat at the table after we've cleared up. (*She and* NETTA *go*)

HARLEY (*On phone*): Hi, toots, I'm still here. No, I won't be long. I'll tell 'em. You keep your seams straight.

BUDDY: Boy, I thought that girl was gonna start wrecking the furniture in here. Who the devil is she?

ELDON: From what she said, you know perfectly well who she is.

BUDDY: You're the one who was talking to her. Let me in here, I'd have handled it.

ELDON: Sounds like you've been handling it all along.

HARLEY: I don't know what happens with that kind of girl. They paint up what could be a pretty face, twist their behinds around. Can't be more than seventeen years old, already she's the worst whore in town. She is.

BUDDY: Hot number like that could be trouble.

ELDON: No, no, no trouble. She's going to be no problem.

BUDDY: No problem of mine.

ELDON: That depends on whose story you believe.

BUDDY: Shoot, every guy in town's been down to those woods. Maybe she got me mixed up with Timmy.

ELDON: No more of that.

BUDDY: No more of what?

ELDON: No more of that anymore. That's all over now.

BUDDY: What's over?

ELDON: You think everything you do is all right, if you can drag Timmy into it.

BUDDY: I never used Tim for anything in my life. There's not two brothers in town closer than—

ELDON: Fine, I know. I know.

BUDDY: Those doors are thick, but that girl wasn't talking all that private. You gonna lecture me about moral weakness and character? Like Granddad?

ELDON: That's enough.

BUDDY (*Easy*): I remember all those lectures about moral fiber. I used to think you ought to order a couple hundred bolts, make you a new line of clothes outta moral fiber.

HARLEY: Shit. They wouldn't move. Sit on the shelves and go begging.

(LOTTIE *enters*)

BUDDY: Good Lord, Aunt Lottie. Thought you'd gone to bed.

LOTTIE: I don't go to bed, you know that.

ELDON: Are you all right?

LOTTIE: I swear to God, Eldon, I feel like I might glow in the dark.

ELDON: Is that good? I don't think that sounds—

LOTTIE: That's not good. No, that's not good.

ELDON: Lottie—Buddy. How are we supposed to take this? How do people take it?

LOTTIE: I don't know, Eldon.

ELDON: I can't get Netta to talk about it. I don't think it's really hit her yet.

(*The radio has been turned on*)

ELDON: No, don't turn that on, damn fool thing, what do I care tonight what's happening with the war? I got my—one son here with me. My other, I don't even know where he fell. I just wish I knew that he got his man.

BUDDY: You can be damned sure Tim did.

ELDON: Ten for one, damn them, and they keep fighting. That's what the paper says, ten Japs for one Yank.

HARLEY: You can be damn sure Timmy got his limit, Eldon.

ELDON: I know that; enough of that, now. Enough of that. Has Sally come in?

LOTTIE: I haven't heard her.

ELDON: She still doesn't know. Well . . . we've got Buddy here.

BUDDY: Yeah, I wish I was here for good.

HARLEY: We'll have you back down at that plant before you know it.

BUDDY: Oh boy. Maybe I'll stay in Italy.

HARLEY: See, he's seeing the world, he starts getting ideas.

ELDON: How you gonna keep them down on the farm? Huh? After they've seen—well, Rome, I guess it has to be.

BUDDY: Naw, I'm like Granddad. I'm not stuck on that factory.

ELDON: I know; I've never forced it on you.

BUDDY: No, sir. Come home from Princeton with a degree in business administration; in a week I'm fixing sewing machines.

HARLEY: Still the best repairman we've had down there.

ELDON: I seem to remember it wasn't long before you were working at the bank.

BUDDY: You know it.

ELDON: Hell, I own what, a quarter of that bank. I never could stand it.

BUDDY: To each his own. I can't believe I'm back. No wonder they don't want us coming home on leave. If it wasn't for Timmy, this would be . . . (*He nearly cries, recovers, tries to continue heartily*) Boy! I tell you, after last winter, I'm trying to convince Olive to live in a desert somewhere. California or Arizona. I mean it rained—and cold.

ELDON: I always imagined Italy to be warm.

BUDDY: Yeah, sunny Italy, what a load of fertilizer that is. Hell, when the ground froze, at least you could walk on it. You've never seen so many kids in your life. We learned to say to them, "*Buon giorno, ragazzo*," and they're supposed to say, "*Bene grassi, signor.*" You know what they say?

HARLEY: What's that?

BUDDY: "Got any gum, chum?"

ELDON: Sounds like Clark balled up Italy as much as Nimitz did the Pacific.

BUDDY: I don't know what else General Clark was supposed to do. I just counted myself lucky to be in out of the rain.

(TALLEY *enters, dragging a large, half-filled mailbag*)

ELDON: I thought you were in your room.

TALLEY (*Lucid*): No, no. Kenneth.

BUDDY: Sir.

TALLEY: Harley. Good evening. I'm surprised you're showing your face, Eldon.

ELDON: Did the women get you something to eat?

TALLEY: Yes, thank you, I've had sufficient. Is Emmet Young back yet?

ELDON: I didn't know he'd gone someplace.

TALLEY: Kenneth, bring along that big sack full of papers to the kitchen.

BUDDY: Yes, sir.

ELDON: Dad, we should go through anything that's important together.

TALLEY: Now listen here—if I have to talk to you. There's some papers nobody's business but mine—long useless to anybody but me—that I intend to burn in the kitchen cook stove. If that's all the same to everybody. You just tend to your sewing machines, that's always suited you fine, and suited me fine.

ELDON: Dad, you might destroy something that . . .

TALLEY: Sir, that's all, sir. (*He exits*)

ELDON (*Sotto voce*): What got his dander up?

LOTTIE: He's just covering his tracks like a good fox.

TALLEY (*Coming back*): I think you'll find a fox doubles back on his tracks, he doesn't cover them up, Charlotte. (*To* BUDDY) Go on, then, and poke those a few at a time into the stove there.

(BUDDY *exits*)

HARLEY: Buddy.

TALLEY: Mind you don't get yourself burned.

HARLEY: Well, hell.

ELDON: I'd like to go through those things with you.

TALLEY: You been digging through everything in there like a dog for a mole. Nothing that would interest anybody but me, thank you. (*Starts to go*)

HARLEY: Old love letters, maybe.

TALLEY (*Turns*): No, sir, I left the loving everybody except my wife to your father, Mr. Campbell. And my son, here. And you see where that's got us. Small mind in business and adulterous in his marriage, and everybody in the state knows it.

ELDON: There's no call to speak to that now, Dad. (*Sotto voce*) Boy, I can't take this tonight.

TALLEY: How many girls—

LOTTIE: Not tonight, Dad.

TALLEY: —was it you came to me about before you was shipped off to school? Who was the New Jersey lawyer sent here to sue you for parentage? He didn't know who he was dealing with, I can tell you. Sent him packing.

ELDON: And used it as an excuse to pull me out of school two months before I graduated.

TALLEY: Set you up, sir, in business down there—only place I knew of where I wouldn't have to lay eyes on you.

ELDON: And I took that two-bit outfit and made it into something you should be proud of.

TALLEY: Pride goeth before the fall, sir. I was your age exactly when the Great War came. I saw it coming. You looked at Europe, you looked at the Pacific, said it wouldn't happen again. Anybody could have told you better and did. With that son-of-a-bitch Democrat cripple in the White House playing king, roughshodding over every good man in the country till he decided he needed them to fight his war.

HARLEY: All that's changing now; things aren't going to be that easy for him.

TALLEY: I saw what was coming in 1914. You stuck your head in the sand.

LOTTIE: You bought everything the war was gonna use and sold it back to them for double, didn't you, Papa?

TALLEY: Yes, I did, and treble and four times, and it bought you the college education you never used and the food in your mouth and the shirt on your back, young man, and don't you forget it.

LOTTIE: I'm not a young man anymore, Papa.

TALLEY: Well, Lottie, if you didn't tell them, there wouldn't be nobody who'd know the difference.

LOTTIE: At this point, if I recall the last time he was quasi-coherent, he begins on how frail and beautiful Momma was and his disappointment in me. Very reminiscent of Eldon's lament over Sally. (*She stands up, is dizzy, and is forced to sit back down*) Well, so much for the grand gesture. I was intending to sweep from the room.

TALLEY: That's the only sweeping you'd know how to do, Charlotte. Fine children I raised. You and what's-his-name both. If Stuart had lived, then you'da seen something—

ELDON: That's fine, Dad, don't get excited.

LOTTIE: You had one die and two that were stillborn, Daddy, and none of us asked for the favor of having you for a father.

ELDON: That's enough, Lottie.

LOTTIE (*Lower*): I never could understand why he kept trying if he was so unhappy with us.

ELDON (*Low*): Maybe he wanted to keep at it till he got another one he was satisfied with.

LOTTIE: Well, Momma, bless her, didn't live that long. Doctors told him she wasn't strong enough; it's not like we're Catholic. Didn't they have rubbers back at the turn of the century?

ELDON: Lottie, for God's sake.

LOTTIE: I don't know why I'd expect you to know—you're apparently completely unacquainted with them.

TALLEY: Eldon.

ELDON: Dad?

TALLEY: Who? I don't want to be in this room.

ELDON: Are you O.K.?

TALLEY: Blamed! Where's the boy? Where's Eldon?

ELDON: I'm right here.

TALLEY: Where?

ELDON: Who? Goddamn it, now he's got me doing it.

TALLEY: The boy.

ELDON: Kenneth is in the kitchen, where you sent him. (*Pause*) Dad? What's wrong?

TALLEY: My God, sir, what I've come to . . .

ELDON: You're better than last week—if you'd take care of yourself. You shouldn't be trying to do all this. If you'd let me help.

TALLEY: Where?

ELDON: Where's what?

TALLEY: Your boy.

ELDON: You had Buddy take a sack of papers to burn in the cooking stove that hasn't been connected for twenty years. Nora cooks on an oil range now.

TALLEY: Then we'll take them out to the barnyard, sir. (*Exits. Pause*)

ELDON: And there's no barnyard either.

HARLEY: He starts in with the "sirs" and "thank you's" and you're in trouble.

ELDON: I hope he's not burning anything important—you never know with him.

HARLEY: Well, before I go, you know what I'm going to say.

ELDON: Not tonight, Harley.

HARLEY: Eldon, I was willing to wait till Timmy got back.

ELDON: Not tonight.

HARLEY: It's not going to be any easier tomorrow.

ELDON: I know that, thank you.

HARLEY: Buddy's here, you're here.

ELDON: You want to explain it to Dad? And why we're not waiting for Timmy? You want to tell him that?

HARLEY: Anything to do with that plant, you don't need him. You got power of attorney.

ELDON: Well, that wasn't my idea, that was the government's idea. I'd never use it. It isn't funny, Lottie.

LOTTIE: Government man came down here to tell Dad how good Talley & Son was doing and Dad kept calling the factory a chicken farm.

ELDON: He was pretty bad that year.

HARLEY (*Laughs*): Told the inspector to pick out a pair of hens to take home for himself.

ELDON: Now look at him; the man has nine lives. No disrespect. His father died at thirty. Built this house and didn't live a year in it. I think Dad lived out his dad's life and then his own. And then mine.

OLIVE (*Entering*): Now, it's absolutely against my principles to indulge you men like this, but Mother says if you come into the kitchen and get your coffee, you can bring it back in the parlor. We're not finished in the kitchen yet. Aunt Charlotte, there's a good apple pie . . .

BUDDY (*Entering*): Dad.

ELDON: Anything important in those papers?

BUDDY: I don't think so.

OLIVE: No, no, don't come in without your coffee, and there's pie. Get it in the kitchen and bring it in here.

HARLEY: What kind of service is that? We're trying to talk in here. I thought you'd bring it in on a fancy tray.

OLIVE: We happen not to have a maid anymore, like you do, Harley. And I'm not going to volunteer. Wouldn't I look cute— I'll get me a little hat and sew a little ruffle around my apron.

HARLEY: I remember when you had a maid and a girl to help Nora out.

OLIVE: Well, that was before my time. Try to find a colored girl now with the wages they're getting down at your factory. Aunt Lottie, you're going to go straight to H–E–double-tooth-picks with those cards.

LOTTIE: Oh, kiss my ass.

OLIVE: Well, you'd enjoy that, wouldn't you! Why are you so hateful to me?

BUDDY: Honey.

ELDON: Ladies. Olive, Lottie isn't well tonight.

OLIVE: Eldon, I understand sorrow and tension. I told Lottie she looked upset and tired; she should go to bed.

ELDON: She hasn't been sleeping.

LOTTIE: I've never slept. Maybe I'm bored, not tired.

OLIVE: Well, I don't understand that as something to be proud of.

BUDDY: Olive.

OLIVE: Well, don't "Olive" me, dernit. I don't understand being bored and I don't understand not being able to sleep. I understand getting up early and working hard and getting things done and being tired and going to sleep and sleeping.

BUDDY: Honey?

OLIVE: And getting up early and working hard and getting things done and being tired and going to sleep and sleeping. There's too much to do to be bored, and there's too much to do not to be tired, and there's too much to do not to sleep. I'm sorry, that's the way I am. It's the way I am. That's the way I am.

ELDON: Come on.

BUDDY: Honey!

ELDON: Come on, sweetheart.

(*She exits,* BUDDY *and* ELDON *follow*)

HARLEY: Buddy. Eldon. (*He exits, leaving* LOTTIE *and* TIMMY *onstage*)

TIMMY: Dad said he didn't even know where I fell. That official "fell." Like a lotta people he gets very—not just correct, but formal—under pressure. Hell, "fell" isn't the half of it. Splatted is more like it. Didn't feel a thing. Shock and whatnot takes care of that. I felt a force all against me and suddenly I've got a different angle on the terrain. I'm looking up into the trees instead of out across the jungle floor. I thought, How am I looking at that? Then I thought, Oh, sure, I'm flat on my ass looking up. Some squawking parrot up there looking down at me; gonna drop it right on my face. I figgered, all right, this part is easy. I just lay here till some corpsman comes up and does his job. You get very philosophical. Then the corpsmen come and, oh, Daddy, I knew from the look on their faces that this is bad. This young recruit, couldn't be sixteen, turned around and I thought he was gonna puke, but he flat out fainted before he had the chance. You could tell he'd enlisted in this thing ten minutes after seeing *To the Shores of Tripoli.* Then all of a sudden I'm on a stretcher and they're rushing me off to somewhere. You understand, you don't feel the stretcher under you, you just know they're rushing you to somewhere.

You're looking up into the sun; some guy is running along beside you, trying to keep his hand over your eyes, shade them from the sun; you'd kinda rather see it. And all the corpsmen are still looking so cut-up I said, "Hey, do you raggedy-asses think I don't know you're razzing me? I got a pass to go home, you're trying to make me think I won't get there." Or, actually, I thought I said that; then I realized nothing had come out. I thought, Well, hell, if this isn't a lousy predicament. You always wondered if it comes will you fall all to pieces, and now it's come and I'm doing fine and damned proud of it and nobody is gonna know. (TALLEY *enters from the kitchen and exits out the front door*) Granddad Talley would say, "Pride goeth before a fall, sir." Should have known it. Of course, you do know that the body is doing what the body does. You can feel—barely, a little bit—that your body is urinating all over itself and your bowels are letting go something fierce. You try to get ahold with your mind of the muscles down in your belly that you use to hold it off, but your mind can't find 'em. (*Pause*) If those guys hadn't looked so bad, you might have gone all to pieces, but they're so torn up, you feel somebody has got to take this thing lightly.

NETTA (*Off*): Eldon.

ELDON (*Enters; NETTA following*): I wish you wouldn't hound me tonight, damn it.

NETTA: I just want to know what that woman was doing here. I wouldn't put it past her to take something from the house.

ELDON: I don't know who you're talking about.

NETTA: That Viola Platt. I don't want her coming around.

ELDON: She's been doing the wash here for fifteen years—

NETTA: And I've never liked it a minute and I've never trusted her a minute. I'd rather do the washing myself or, God knows, there's any number of colored women into Old Town who need the money more than she does. Her husband just drinks it up and gives us all a bad name.

ELDON: I want to say right now that I've had it with this hysterical attitude you and Olive have tonight— We're all upset, but there's no call for this.

NETTA: There is call and I'm calling, and Olive is with me in this. Now, I'm just shaking like a leaf, this has got me so upset.

ELDON: Please get it through your head that it means nothing to me who does the washing here.

NETTA: Then we understand each other fine. But can you tell me why she's come back here again three times now in one day?

ELDON: Where? What's she doing here?

NETTA: Emmet drove her to the front of the house; your father went out personally to—

TALLEY (*Entering with* EMMET *and* VIOLA): In here. Here. If you please. I asked Mr. Young if he would be so kind as to fetch Mrs. Platt here. I want to thank the both of you for coming by at this hour.

ELDON: Dad, not tonight. I'm sorry, Mrs. Platt, we've had some bad news here—

TALLEY: Mrs. Platt, Mr. Young, I think you're acquainted . . . ?

VIOLA: I know who he is, I guess; we ain't acquainted.

NETTA: Mr. Talley, I'm about at the end of my patience here.
I want you to please explain to—

TALLEY: This is a family thing that we can have you join us
for or not. If you'd rather, you can please shut the door behind
you. (NETTA *looks at* ELDON *and leaves, shutting the door*)
This won't be but a minute.

ELDON: Dad, no. Whatever you're up to. Not tonight.

TALLEY: I heard you the first time, sir. You can sit over there
and attend or join the women in the kitchen. I imagine these
two people want to get home.

VIOLA: It sure ain't my preference to be hauled out of the
house in the middle of the night.

TALLEY: Now, the past is the past and we're not going to talk
about that. I think we know why we're here. Now, Viola, your
daughter—her name is . . . ?

VIOLA: Avalaine?

TALLEY: Speak up, Platt; say what?

VIOLA: Avalaine, Mr. Talley.

TALLEY: Avalaine.

VIOLA: I thought she'd runned off.

TALLEY: Well, it's turned out that that is not the case. Now,
I am a man who has always been direct and fair, anybody will
testify.

LOTTIE: God save us!

TALLEY: Charlotte, you look terrible. You should be in bed.

LOTTIE: Not on your life.

VIOLA: Avalaine said she come up here and got slapped in the face for her trouble. I tried to talk to Mr. Eldon, but you being so busy—

TALLEY: Your daughter stated a slander in this house this afternoon, which won't happen again.

VIOLA: Avalaine most often says what she likes.

(*There is a commotion in the hall*)

AVALAINE (*Off*): You just get your damn hands off me—(*Opening the door*) Is Ma in here?

OLIVE (*From doorway*): Mr. Talley is in a private—

AVALAINE: I said somethin's going on, goddamn it, and I'm gonna know what it is.

OLIVE: Mr. Talley, Mr. Eldon—

AVALAINE: Are you talkin' about me?

ELDON: I don't want this commotion, now.

AVALAINE: It don't much matter what you want. Mom, what're they saying here?

NETTA: Eldon—

TALLEY: That's fine.

ELDON: That's fine, Dad said. I don't know what—

TALLEY: Miss Platt, I thought you'd be contrite and embarrassed, or I would have asked you to join us. (*Pause.* AVALAINE *looks at him*) Maybe she is.

AVALAINE: I don't know what you're talking "embarrassed." You got something to say, say it.

ELDON: You're opening a can of beans you've no—

TALLEY: Eldon, shut the door if you would.

(AVALAINE *flinches when* ELDON *approaches*)

ELDON: I'm not going to hit you. (*He closes the door*)

AVALAINE (*To* EMMET): What the hell are you doing here?

EMMET: Would you just shut up.

AVALAINE: We's supposed to go to the picture show.

TALLEY: Now, one thing has to be understood. Avalaine Platt, you stated a slander in this house this afternoon; that won't happen again.

AVALAINE: I didn't say nothin' that wasn't the—

EMMET: Why don't you listen once?

TALLEY: We don't have to worry about you repeating it, as that would be actionable by lawsuit.

AVALAINE: Bullshit.

TALLEY: The Jeff City jails aren't so full they can't take a few more; not just you, but whoever in your family is spreading this libel. I don't have to go into that. As it happens, I've been

talking to Mr. Young here for some time. Mr. Young is inti-
mately acquainted with Avalaine, which I assume you know.

VIOLA: I guess if that means what I think it means, I ain't
surprised. It's no business of yours.

TALLEY: Say what?

VIOLA: I know she likes the soldier boys.

TALLEY: Mr. Young is very much a civilian.

AVALAINE: He's got asthma.

EMMET: I got flat feet.

TALLEY: Now, I've asked that he join us here because Mr.
Young applied for the job of cutter at the factory last month,
wanting, as he said, a position that had more of a future. Inside,
out of the weather. Mr. Young is an ambitious man. Now, my
son had thought of hiring another applicant, but tonight we've
made the decision that Mr. Young is the right man for that
position. Now, I think you wanted to say something.

EMMET: It's been put to me that Avalaine and I should be
married.

AVALAINE: In a pig's eye.

TALLEY: I think that would be the honorable thing for the
young Mr. Young and Miss Platt to do. And I'm happy that
we'll be giving you the means to do the honorable thing. I
don't see any other way we could accept them into our home.

EMMET: I understand that, sir. Sirs. (*To* AVALAINE) What'd I
tell you?

TALLEY: Then I think Eldon will agree that you can start at the factory as a wedding present. The day after the marriage takes place. I feel it's the least I can offer, Miss Platt, and, if you understand me, it's the most I can offer.

AVALAINE: Oh, it ain't difficult to understand. It just ain't enough.

VIOLA: If that's all you wanted, you should have asked Avalaine here to begin with.

ELDON: It's not necessary, Dad.

VIOLA: I ain't asked nothin' from nobody, I want that understood.

ELDON: I know that, Viola.

VIOLA: I tried to tell you.

ELDON: I know.

VIOLA: You people don't owe us.

AVALAINE: Like hell they don't—

VIOLA: You don't have to do nothin' you don't want to, Avie. You can just as easy go to Springfield.

AVALAINE: On what?

TALLEY: Thank you very much. With Miss Platt here, I think we'll do fine.

VIOLA: If I tell you, you just do different out of spite.

TALLEY: Thank you very much. (*Pause*) Thank you very much.

LOTTIE: That means he's finished with you, honey.

VIOLA: Is that what that means? Avie don't have to do nothin' she don't want.

LOTTIE: No, she doesn't.

AVALAINE: I ain't said nothin'—one way or another—

VIOLA: Well, none of that work is gonna finish itself. (ELDON *gets up*) Don't you bother, Mr. Eldon. I know the way out of this house. (*She exits*)

TALLEY: Mr. Young, congratulations. Eldon, she said she can find the door. I know we none of us will have to think about this again.

AVALAINE: I ain't said nothin', I said.

EMMET: Will you listen once?

AVALAINE: Will you jump in the lake.

EMMET: He could have you in jail in a minute.

AVALAINE: Like hell he could.

EMMET: The hell he couldn't.

AVALAINE: And have his name in the paper?

EMMET: They wouldn't print it, nobody'd know.

(*They argue in violent whispers*)

TALLEY: I think we can expect Mr. Young to put it to Miss Platt; he seems inclined that way.

AVALAINE (*To* EMMET): What's to prevent it?

EMMET: Excuse me, sir, but we got no guarantee.

AVALAINE: We sure ain't.

TALLEY: Harley; Eldon, yell for Harley.

ELDON: Emmet, get Harley.

EMMET (*Opening the door*): Mr. Campbell, Mr. Talley wants you in here.

NETTA (*In the doorway*): Has she left?

ELDON: I'm sure you saw her go.

NETTA: Eldon, I want you to tell me why she was up here. Is that girl gone?

AVALAINE: No, I ain't gone.

HARLEY (*Entering*): Yes, sir.

(BUDDY *and* OLIVE *appear in the doorway*)

TALLEY: Mr. Young—Mr. Campbell.

HARLEY: I know Emmet.

TALLEY: Mr. Young will be working alongside us down at the plant.

HARLEY: What do you mean "us"? I haven't seen you down there in twenty years.

TALLEY: Beside you and Eldon. Soon as the wedding's over. I just wanted you to meet here in this house, to start you two boys off on the right foot. Now, these two young people have to run along.

EMMET: Of course, the job of cutter isn't much of a—

ELDON: Bribe.

EMMET: —incentive.

AVALAINE: Cuttin'-room foreman might be more attractive.

HARLEY: You're joking. Cutter takes home over two hundred bucks a week. That's more than me or Eldon, either one draws.

(*Pause*)

AVALAINE: Mr. Talley? Cuttin'-room foreman?

TALLEY: For your first anniversary present.

ELDON: Dad, Harley's the man who does the hiring and fir- ing—

TALLEY: Sir. You never admit when you've been outsmarted, and I do.

EMMET: If that could be in writing.

AVALAINE: I want to see all you said in writing. I can read.

TALLEY: Tomorrow morning. You get married tomorrow, I see no reason you can't start work the day after. Now, is that agreeable, Miss Platt?

LOTTIE: That's nothing you have to accept, Avalaine.

AVALAINE: Oh sure, you don't want nobody to have nothin', 'cept you. That's agreeable all except "inviting us into your home." Don't expect me to be spending much time up here.

TALLEY: Whatever you want. Now I'm tired.

LOTTIE: I don't wonder.

EMMET: I want to thank . . .

TALLEY: No thanks, no thanks. That's something you'll earn. And everything that comes after. Both of you.

AVALAINE: Can we leave here now?

TALLEY: Eldon, you want to see these people home?

AVALAINE: Emmet's got a car.

EMMET: Thank you. Good night.

LOTTIE: Good luck.

EMMET: Mrs. Talley.

NETTA: Good night.

EMMET (*To* ELDON): Dad.

(EMMET *and* AVALAINE *leave, squealing as soon as they are out the door*)

OLIVE (*Entering*): Look at the way he dresses. Drives that fancy car. Everyone rationed to three gallons a week, I don't want to think where he gets the stamps for gas.

LOTTIE: You're really slick, huh, Dad?

TALLEY: Heck, it wasn't even fun. Shooting fish in a barrel. (*To* ELDON) You stick it to a sow, you shouldn't be surprised to have a pig offspring; whatsoever a man soweth, that shall he also reap.

LOTTIE: If that was true, Daddy, I don't want to think what you'd be also reaping.

TALLEY: I'm glad you're not my judge, Charlotte.

LOTTIE: I'll be somewhere lobbying, Daddy.

ELDON: I hope you're happy now, Dad.

TALLEY: I've wiped your nose for you for the last time, sir.

ELDON: I could have taken care of it.

NETTA: What do you mean by that? (TALLEY *exits into office*. *To* ELDON) Do you want to explain that? Do you want to tell us what you could have taken care of.

OLIVE: Dad, do you think—

ELDON: —I'm not joking about you two and your hysterics now.

NETTA: Do I look hysterical to you, Eldon? Because if you don't know what I'm saying, I'm perfectly willing to spell it out. Now you are walking on thin ice through a field of wild oats here and you better watch your step.

LOTTIE: I swear to God, Dad is the craftiest son-of-a-bitch I ever encountered.

NETTA: Yes, he is, Lottie, all of that. He doesn't care what he makes Eldon look like.

ELDON: Hell, that's the only reason he did it.

NETTA: Of course Eldon didn't care what he made us look like.

HARLEY: You think that man can learn the job?

ELDON: Don't you give me a hard time now. What's so difficult about pushing a cutting saw around a line?

HARLEY: You mess up, you're cutting twelve dozen legs at one go. That could get pretty costly on a narrow profit margin like we're running.

ELDON: Please don't tell me how the cutting room is run, I've cut enough—

HARLEY: You think he's foreman material?

ELDON: We can find something for him to do.

HARLEY: That's my partner who cares so much about the quality of the Talley & Son product.

ELDON: Goddamn it, Harley, we can find something.

HARLEY: I just wanted to know you felt good about it.

ELDON: It'll work out. Don't worry about it.

HARLEY: 'Cause I don't. I guess I'm not stupid. I know what's happening, but I'm damned if I feel good about it. You may think we can find a place for him; I don't think we can.

TALLEY (*At the office door*): Here, Netta. Where's that pie?

NETTA: Olive, see what Mr. Talley wants.

TALLEY: Where is the pie?

OLIVE: I'll get it for you, Granddad. Is there any left?

BUDDY: Sure. (OLIVE *exits*) Better get some of that before it's gone. Harley? (*He and* HARLEY *exit*)

NETTA: It's a great pleasure washing dishes with Olive out in the kitchen talking about getting a new flag for the window with a gold star for Timmy and a blue one for Buddy.

ELDON: Come on, now. None of that talk.

NETTA: I don't want it; I don't want either one of those stars in the window anymore. And I don't want a military funeral with a flag on the casket.

ELDON (*Quite hot*): That can wait till they send our son home. (*He exits to kitchen*)

NETTA: Don't run out when I talk to you.

OLIVE (*Bringing in the pie*): Granddaddy! (*She knocks on office door;* TALLEY *takes the pie and slams the door*) You said you wanted it. Mother. (NETTA *exits; to* LOTTIE) I don't mean to be angry, Lottie. It's not easy for me sometimes.

LOTTIE: Don't pay any attention to me, honey.

(OLIVE *exits*)

TIMMY: Lottie, she's coming up on the porch.

HARLEY (*Off*): I know, I know. All I'm saying.

(SALLY *enters from the door and starts up the stairs*)

ELDON (*Off*): There's no need to raise your voice, now—

LOTTIE: Sally! (SALLY *hasn't heard*) Sally!

HARLEY (*Off*): —not to make too big a fuss about it; all I'm saying is we're doing damn important work down there, and turning a pretty penny doing it. I don't want some green field hand—some mechanic—

SALLY (*Listening to* HARLEY *and* ELDON): I started to say I can't believe they're still yelling, but I should be used to it by now.

ELDON (*Off*): There's no call to get angry. If we can't talk—

HARLEY (*Off*): Sure, sure, fine. I don't want a wrench thrown in it, Eldon, is all I'm saying.

LOTTIE: Matt Friedman was down at the boathouse, wasn't he?

SALLY: Yes.

LOTTIE: I knew that's where he'd go. Soon as they said his car was alongside the road. I swear to God, I've been straining my ears so hard I'm damned near deaf.

SALLY: We're going to drive down to Springfield, junk that Plymouth, and take the bus up to St. Louis. I want to tell them I'm leaving.

LOTTIE: No. You're not going to stay another minute here. All hell is breaking loose here tonight.

SALLY: Well, a little more from me'll be good for them.

TIMMY: Don't let her go in the kitchen.

LOTTIE: I won't allow you to go in there. You go in there and I swear to you, Sally, everything will change. You won't be able to get on that bus.

SALLY: I thought you knew me better than that.

LOTTIE: Sally, I been keeping alive to hear this and you aren't going to spoil it for either one of us now.

SALLY: I swear you'd think it was you running off.

LOTTIE: It is, it is me. I been courting that crazy person all winter long. Now I'm running off to St. Louis and getting married.

SALLY: I have no bitterness, Aunt Lottie. They can't touch me tonight.

LOTTIE: If you got no bitterness, then you got no need. You— Oh damn, what did Mrs. Platt tell Avalaine? She didn't have sense enough to do it. You got sense, I hope.

TIMMY: "Fly away on."

LOTTIE: She told her, "You fly away on," so now I'm telling you: "You fly away on."

SALLY: I don't know how fast a Trailways bus is gonna fly.

LOTTIE: Fast enough. High enough.

HARLEY (*In hallway, to* BUDDY): You just finish your pie and come on in here.

SALLY: I have to pack some things. If you don't want me to see them, then I better go.

ELDON: I'd as soon thrash all this out tomorrow.

LOTTIE: Sneak up quick. Run upstairs.

HARLEY: The old man's here, you're here, Buddy's here.

ELDON: I know.

HARLEY: I'm not going back to the telegraph office anymore. I tell you. I'd rather it'd been anybody on this earth come to you with that news than me.

(*They open the front door and step out*)

SALLY: What?

SALLY: There hasn't anything happened, has there? What's happened?

LOTTIE: Oh, Sally. Your brother . . .

TIMMY: Don't you dare.

LOTTIE: He's just been raising hell. You know how Buddy . . . Nothing you have to hear tonight. Run upstairs. You call me tomorrow and I'll tell you everything.

SALLY: You tell them where I've gone. (*She gives* LOTTIE *a hug*)

LOTTIE: Oh, I'll tell them, don't think I won't.

(HARLEY *and* ELDON *come back in*)

HARLEY: They've started the Fourth of July celebration down by the river.

LOTTIE: Go go go go go go go go. (*She opens the double doors and pushes* SALLY, *as* ELDON *and* HARLEY *come in the other double doors*) Oh, I could just dance a jig. I could just dance a jig. Damn me for never learning how to dance a jig.

ELDON: You look like the cat that ate the canary.

LOTTIE: Do I look like that? I got to admit that's the way I feel. I chopped down the cherry tree and I ate the canary. Sweetest little thing I ever et. Tasted like lemon-meringue pie. Everybody knew they tasted like that, there wouldn't be a canary left in this town.

BUDDY (*Entering*): Harley!

HARLEY: Sit down, sit down. We should just go over the Delaware proposal step by step, I guess.

OLIVE (*Entering*): I didn't know if you'd need these brochures or not.

TALLEY (*Comes from office, pie in hand*) Harley, before you go. (*Hands the pie to* OLIVE) Here. This ain't got no taste.

OLIVE: I beg your pardon. I put a full teaspoon of nutmeg and two teaspoons of cinnamon in that pie. (NETTA *enters*)

HARLEY: Good to see you so fit, sir, but all due respect, I'm the man does the hiring down there, and I'm not so sure you're recruiting the right man for the job.

TALLEY: Never had any intention of that fool working down there. I wouldn't have him around. Now, sir. This is the note, and this is the partnership agreement signed by me and your dad. This is the certificate of ownership on that factory. (*To* OLIVE) That say ownership?

ELDON: That's what I thought he was up to all along.

OLIVE: Yes, sir, it does.

TALLEY: Now, tomorrow after that baboon and his concubine get married, you call up your Delaware people and you tell them to go ahead with that takeover. After they move that equipment down to Baton Rouge, Mr. Young can do all the cutting and all the foremanning he wants. Let *them* find out what they got. But he ain't working one day for me. Now I'm going to bed.

HARLEY: You don't sell the plant because you got someone working for you you don't like.

NETTA: You do if you want to get rid of a scandal. You send 'em to a town that never heard of the Talleys.

TALLEY: I've never been blackmailed and I won't be. Not by some whore of Whistler's here.

NETTA: Of Eldon's, you mean.

ELDON: I think you'll find the Talley share of that factory is mine, and that decision is mine.

TALLEY: You try not to talk, 'cause I'm making an effort to make sense—we know how I get. I went into that office and prayed for the soul of my grandson, Timothy Everett Talley, who isn't coming back from the Pacific.

LOTTIE: Dear Jesus.

TALLEY: Those two were going to get it all. Now there's just one and he don't want no part of it and never did, and I don't either and never did. Now, Harley, are you for that takeover; yes or no?

HARLEY: If we can work it out.

TALLEY: Good. Here, what's-your-name, vote on the takeover. Yes or no. Move it out or keep it here. The Talleys are voting on what's going to happen to their share of that pestilent place.

BUDDY: We've been talking about it, sir; I've just been listening.

OLIVE: Buddy, honey, come here a—

TALLEY: You're no namby-pamby; if you are, you grow up now.

BUDDY: There's a lot of things I'd rather do.

OLIVE: Buddy.

BUDDY: You know my interest in the bank, sir.

TALLEY: Speak your mind, what there is of it.

ELDON: Don't let him badger you, Son.

BUDDY: It means a lot to Dad, sir. You better sit down.

TALLEY: Takeover, yes or no, if you want your share. Otherwise I'll give the blamed thing to what's-his-name. Yes or no? Yes or no?

BUDDY: Yes.

OLIVE: Darn it, Buddy.

TALLEY: So. We've had a democratic vote like a family. I vote for them, Kenneth votes for them, you vote for yourself and lose. Two to one. Now, Harley, you know what we think— you do what you want about it.

BUDDY: Dad, I'm sorry, I've never wanted to work there.

TALLEY: Don't be sorry.

OLIVE: Mr. Talley, sit down.

TALLEY: Sorry is for people who know they're doing the wrong thing while they're doing it. You ask Eldon about sorry.

ELDON: Yeah, I could tell you a lot.

HARLEY: If the factory is worth somebody wanting it, it's only because of the standards you've—

ELDON: I'm glad you understand that.

HARLEY: We'll thrash this out tomorrow. It's your decision really, not . . . (*Nods to* TALLEY)

ELDON: I know it is. Dad doesn't know it. I guess Buddy doesn't either.

BUDDY: What's that?

ELDON: Olive knows though, don't you? I have to say, Buddy, I'm a little surprised.

BUDDY: Dad, I'd like to be down there with you like Timmy was, but . . .

ELDON: No, you always liked going off with your grandpa to the bank.

BUDDY: I did, sir.

ELDON: And you expect a position to be waiting there for you when you get out, I know. You remember back when my momma died, she left, what was it, thirty percent of the bank to Dad and thirty to me?

BUDDY: Yes, sir.

ELDON: She wanted to be sure I had something, I guess. I've never seen Dad so mad in my life. Remember that, Dad? Tried to get a lawyer to overthrow the will.

OLIVE: Don't get him upset, Dad, he's just burning up.

ELDON: You have what, Harley—twenty-two percent of the bank?

HARLEY: Last time I looked.

ELDON: Now, I figure it's worth about half of the Talley share of that factory, right?

HARLEY: About that, maybe a little more.

TALLEY: No, sir. That factory cannot be touched. Not by you.

ELDON (*To* HARLEY): I know I'll be taking a punishing loss, Harley, but if you're willing, I'd just as soon swap your share in the bank for the Talley half of that factory.

BUDDY: Dad, now . . .

HARLEY: I couldn't let you do that, Eldon.

TALLEY: Not yours to give and not yours to deal, sir.

ELDON: No, Dad, for over two years I've had power of attorney.

TALLEY: You got no power of nothin' over me.

ELDON: I never dreamed I'd use it. Never dreamed it.

TALLEY: No lawyer on this earth—

ELDON: Dad, damn it, the government man came here to talk to you about increasing production down there, you told him if the hens weren't laying to wring their necks.

LOTTIE: He told you to put more girls on the line, you said you'd put twenty of 'em to set on a dozen eggs each.

ELDON: Then you went around the house crowing like a rooster for two weeks. Harley, swap me your part of the bank.

BUDDY: Dad, we'd be losing our shirts on a trade like that.

HARLEY: You'd want a considerable piece of change, Eldon, I'm not that liquid right now.

ELDON: Thank you, no, not a nickel. With Timmy gone I've got no further interest in the garment business. We'll just shake on it and draw up the papers tomorrow. Yes or no?

HARLEY: You're putting me on the spot here.

ELDON: Yes or no? It's the only way. Your part of the bank for our part of Talley & Son.

OLIVE: That doesn't seem really—

ELDON: That's all right, Olive.

OLIVE: Well, it isn't fair to us, is it?

ELDON: Everybody's all of a sudden worried about what's right and fair. Harley, I've never known you to hesitate over a bargain. You gonna start waffling? Where's that natural greed, boy?

TALLEY: That's my bank down there.

ELDON: No, Dad, it was part mine and part yours; now it's going to be all mine. Harley?

HARLEY: I'll go along with you, Eldon, if that's what you want.

ELDON: Good. I'll see you in the morning then.

OLIVE: I tried to tell you, Buddy.

HARLEY: Good night, Mrs. Talley.

NETTA: Good night, Harley.

HARLEY: Uh . . . well, listen, Buddy . . . uh . . . good to see you . . . uh . . . you take care of . . . uh . . . good night all. (*He exits*)

ELDON: I'm sorry, Buddy. I'm sorry, Dad. I know what that bank meant to you two.

OLIVE (*To* BUDDY): Honey, give me a hand with these cups.

ELDON: You and Buddy were going to hear the band.

BUDDY: Not tonight.

ELDON: No, you go on—let your wife show off her soldier in his uniform.

OLIVE: We've got tomorrow night. Mr. Talley?

TALLEY: Face is burning up. Seeing two of everything. Blamed. Seeing two Lotties, two Eldons, two Olives, enough to give a man a heart attack.

BUDDY: Get him a washrag.

(OLIVE *exits*)

TALLEY: I'm fine, sir. I'm fine.

BUDDY: You're gonna lose thousands of dollars on that deal, just out of spite.

ELDON: Well, I can't think of a better way to spend money. You didn't want to get your hands dirty with me and Timmy down at the factory, now you don't have to worry about it.

(OLIVE *comes in with a washcloth*. TALLEY *wipes his face*)

BUDDY: That's enough about Timmy. I'm a little sick of hearing that tonight.

ELDON: Timmy was there. I could count on him. You were never on my side in your life.

BUDDY: Oh, bullshit. All Tim ever did was whatever you wanted, so you'd maybe pat him on the head—which you never did. Timmy was his father's little puppy dog, just like you are.

ELDON: Enough!

BUDDY: God knows, I tried to shake some sense into him. Now the son-of-a-bitch's even died for you. (ELDON *slaps him across the face. The blow is blocked, but* BUDDY *staggers back*) Maybe you'll finally give him credit for doing something.

ELDON: Buddy, you want to work down there at the bank, you better pick up an application tomorrow. There's a lot of good men already ahead of you.

TALLEY: Got no business with that bank, sir.

ELDON: Dad, why don't you go to hell. At least go to bed. You've done enough for one night.

TALLEY: I'm fine, sir.

BUDDY: Let me help you to bed. Come on.

TALLEY: I'm fine, sir.

BUDDY: Come on. Olive, give me a hand. Up you go . . . down you go . . .

(*He helps* TALLEY *out.* OLIVE *follows*)

ELDON (*He takes the washcloth from where* TALLEY *left it, wrings it out in the potted fern. Unconsciously wipes his own face. There is a pause*): You just wonder why you did any of it. Not for Buddy, he was never interested in anything I wanted.

NETTA: I always thought you were doing it for yourself. You knew Buddy didn't like it; I don't think Timmy wanted it either. No point in lying to yourself about it now.

ELDON: I thought they'd see its value when they got older.

NETTA: You didn't care if they did or they didn't as long as you got a day and a half's work out of them. Where the devil has Sally got to?

LOTTIE: I imagine she's around. She'll be here before long.

NETTA: Lottie, don't stay up all night now, you try to get some sleep. (*She is by the window, takes down the flag with two stars*) I don't want this display in the window anymore. I don't want that. And you take down the one that's in the window at the factory, and the one at the bank. I'm going to sleep in Tim's room tonight. Day after tomorrow I'll move my things in there. I'm not getting out of bed tomorrow. I don't want anyone mooning over me; I just want you to know I'm not coming downstairs.

ELDON: There'll be people come tomorrow to pay their respects—

NETTA: I'm not coming downstairs tomorrow. And you tell Buddy I'm not going to the train to see him off, and I'm not writing any more V-mail letters to him in Belgium or France or Italy or wherever they send him. When he comes home, fine, but until he comes home I consider that he's gone, too. I'm not going to sit home and hope he'll be back. (*Pause*) And I want you to lock up the house tonight.

ELDON (*Finding his voice*): Now, no need for that . . .

NETTA (*Still level*): I want the house locked tonight.

ELDON: There's never been a door locked in this town.

NETTA: You shut these windows and you find the keys, wherever they are, and you lock the house. Now I'm going to bed. (*She goes upstairs*)

ELDON: If I lock the doors, I'll lock Sally out.

LOTTIE: I'll be here. (ELDON *would like to say something, but can find nothing to say. He exits to the office as* SALLY *starts to sneak down the stairs. To* SALLY) Wait! (SALLY *goes back up the stairs.* ELDON *re-enters. He goes to the French windows and locks them. He and* LOTTIE *have been shutting off lights as he goes*) Don't forget the windows in the dining room.

ELDON (*Mumbling*): What a bother. (*He goes*)

LOTTIE: (*Calling up the stairs*): Sally!

(SALLY *sneaks down the hall*)

SALLY: We'll have you up to visit us in St. Louis soon as we can.

LOTTIE: No, don't worry about me . . .

SALLY: And we'll be down for a visit next spring. I don't know how the family will like that.

LOTTIE: They'll just have to lump it.

(ELDON *re-enters and stops when he sees* SALLY *and* LOTTIE. SALLY *turns to him*)

SALLY: I'm going to St. Louis tonight.

ELDON: You going to live with that man?

SALLY: I'm going to marry Matt Friedman, yes.

ELDON: It's not like you to run away without telling the family off.

LOTTIE: That was my idea.

ELDON: You sure you're doing the right thing?

SALLY: Oh, I'm sure.

ELDON: Sometimes you think you're doing the right thing but it doesn't work out that way.

SALLY: It'll work out.

ELDON: I hope so, Sally.

(*They embrace*)

LOTTIE: Sally. You call me tomorrow and I want to hear that operator say I have a collect call for Charlotte Talley from Sally Friedman.

SALLY: Goodbye. (*She exits*)

ELDON: She'll call you tomorrow?

LOTTIE: Yes.

ELDON: Someone has to tell her about her brother.

LOTTIE: I'll do that. (*She takes the keys*)

ELDON: Well . . . Good night, Lottie.

LOTTIE: Good night, Mr. Talley. (ELDON *stands for a moment, then exits. Pause.* LOTTIE *and* TIMMY *look out the window*) Dad's right about one thing; everything's gone to the dogs. The house has needed painting for four years.

TIMMY: Yeah, it's beginning to show it. The garden's pretty bad.

LOTTIE: There's no one now to take care of it. (*She unlocks the French windows*)

TIMMY: It's a nice old house. It's a lot smaller than I remember.

LOTTIE (*Opens the French windows—a distant band is playing*) The band's playing down across the river. Oh, that's wonderful. (*A deep breath*) Oh, that's wonderful. What is it, honey?

TIMMY: America won the war today. We all go off; by the time they get back, the country's changed so much I don't imagine they'll recognize it.

LOTTIE: I know.

(TIMMY *walks outside and off.* LOTTIE *stands alone at the windows, listening to the distant band. The music continues as the light fades*)

Curtain

About the Author

Born in Lebanon, Missouri, in 1937, Lanford Wilson grew up in Ozark, Missouri. He attended college in San Diego and Chicago.

Mr. Wilson is a founding member of the Circle Repertory Company in New York. His work at Circle Rep includes *The Hot l Baltimore* (1973), *The Mound Builders* (1975), *Serenading Louie* (1976), *5th of July* (1978), *Talley's Folly* (1980), and *Angels Fall* (1982), all directed by Marshall Mason. His other plays include *The Gingham Dog* (1966), *The Rimers of Eldritch* (1967), *Lemon Sky* (1969), and some twenty produced one-acts. He has also written the libretto for Lee Hoiby's opera of Tennessee Williams's *Summer and Smoke*, and two television plays, *Taxi!* and *The Migrants*.

Mr. Wilson received the 1980 Pulitzer Prize for Drama and the New York Drama Critics' Circle Award for *Talley's Folly*. Other awards include the New York Drama Critics' Circle Award, the Outer Critics' Circle Award and an Obie for *The Hot l Baltimore*, an Obie for *The Mound Builders*, and Tony award nominations for *Talley's Folly*, *5th of July*, and *Angels Fall*. He is the recipient of the Brandeis University Creative Arts Award in Theatre Arts and the Institute of Arts and Letters Award. He is a member of the Dramatists Guild Council.

Mr. Wilson makes his home in Sag Harbor, New York.